Disputed Questions

Disputed Questions
On Being a Christian

Rosemary Radford Ruether

ORBIS BOOKS
Maryknoll, New York 10545

5-23-22

The Catholic Foreign Mission Society of America (Maryknoll) recruits and trains people for overseas missionary service. Through Orbis Books, Maryknoll aims to foster the international dialogue that is essential to mission. The books published, however, reflect the opinions of their authors and are not meant to represent the official position of the society.

ORBIS/ISBN 0-88344-549-2

This book is dedicated to Bea, Betty, Anne, Mimi, Helen, Alice, and Nora: a sisterhood of foremothers.

Contents

Preface to the New Edition

This little book on my intellectual and personal journey of faith and action was written eight years ago in 1981. In this reappearance with Orbis Books I am surprised to find how little I wish to change. It is not that I haven't moved on to additional concerns. Particularly in the area of concern for the theological and social aspects of Palestinian oppression and liberation, my earlier concern with Western anti-semitism has grown an additional arm. To be concerned about relations with Jews, as a Christian, also demands concern for justice to Palestinians.

However, this work on issues of Palestinian rights does not fundamentally change the story of Western Christian responsibility for anti-semitism and the need to rectify that through critical reappraisal of Christian teachings on Christology and the relation of the Church to Judaism. Both on the theological level and on the social level, Christians must make the world hospitable and affirmative to the ongoing creative history of the Jewish people. This commitment for me stands fundamentally unchanged. For this reason I have chosen to leave the section on Christianity and Judaism as it was written seven years ago.

The commitment to justice and hospitality for the Jewish people stands within a fundamental understanding of universalism. Such universalism is based on the assumption that God truly is the God of all people. God is not a Christian, a Jew, or a Muslim. God creates the whole world and is concerned for the well-being of all the creatures within it, humans and others. Christians must interpret their commitment to catholicity non-imperialistically. Thus, we acknowledge that we are not the only "people of God," or the best one, or even the culmination of a process of development, but simply one of God's communities among others.

Christianity has its great gifts to renew for the sake of its own community and to give to others. But these gifts can be received fruitfully only when they are no longer based on concepts of superiority and rights to dominance. This acknowledgment of a true catholicity that is' able to accept other religious communities as peers means that Christianity must reshape its historical relations with Judaism. But it also cannot make that relation compensatory and exclusivist in a way that ignores the oppression of the Palestinian people by Jewish Israeli power. Hope for a redeemed world must begin by saying "never again" will we be silent while any group of people is victimized.

ROSEMARY RADFORD RUETHER

Preamble

Charting one's journey of faith is always a precarious business. One has only limited objectivity about one's own biography. But, even more, one is always, at best, in midjourney. To be more and more fully alive, aware and committed, this is surely the meaning of a journey in faith. But this must mean that we are always reassessing and reappropriating the past—our own past experiences and reflections—in the light of new challenges. A side journey in our spiritual progress, one temporarily shelved, might suddenly become urgent again. In the light of new cultural demands, one might have to look again at some apparently closed questions from one's past to see what is usable. Such might be the case, for example, with my own classical "pagan" background in relation to the challenges of neopagan feminist spirituality, as that movement has developed in recent years. There is a hermeneutic circle with our own past experiences and thoughts, just as with the historical past. What our past means at any given time is always conditioned by the present questions that we bring to it.

In this book I wish to reflect on certain large questions that have shaped my understanding of my social-spiritual identity. In these questions, historical research, theological reflection, and personal meaning have been inextricably interwoven. My excursions into historical research have always been related to questions of personal identity, as a Christian, a Roman Catholic, a woman, an American, white, educated, and "middle class." What does it mean to be those things in a sexist world, an unjust world, a world shaped by religious and racial bigotry, in a church which has too often been on the "wrong side"?

This exploration may be said to follow something of an action-reflection model. I want to look at four large areas that have shaped my thinking; my understanding of my Christian, Catholic, feminist, and American identities. Each of these questions has been generated by large contradictions posed by history and society; by the way history has been shaped by good and bad decisions, and also has been misrepresented by the need of the winners to justify themselves. That shaping of history has resulted in misshaped social relations; between Christians and non-Christians, Christians and Jews, men and women, white and nonwhite, rich and poor. These four areas can be stated as a series of questions or challenges: the question of classical humanism, the question of Jewish faith (as rejection of Christianity), the question of American political society (as a failed promise of national and international justice), and the question of feminism.

In each case I want to discuss some of the ways this challenge has been posed for me by certain experiences, by interactions with ideas and events. I want to show how the experience of particular contradictions has forced me to engage in certain intellectual explorations, and also to situate my identity and my activity in certain ways in response. And, finally, I want to ask how this interaction of experience and reflection has brought me to certain stances of faith. Each of these questions makes Christian existence today highly problematical. They are questions that cannot be solved merely on a theoretical level. They, in turn, pose questions of the credibility and authenticity of one's personal existence. For me none of these questions is closed. Although I have developed certain working positions for responding to them, they are for me open and alive, and must be rethought again and again.

Disputed Questions

1
The Question of
Christian Credibility

Preconditions for Critical Consciousness

In 1954 I entered the freshman class at Scripps
College in Claremont, California. I start my discussion
of my journey in faith there because those years of
undergraduate education were, for me, years of
dramatic intellectual awakening. One might almost
speak of them as years of conversion, from being an
object to being a subject of education, years of being
galvanized into a process of continual, self-motivated
search for enlarged understanding, not as a means of
"winning" something from others, but as a way of
developing and locating myself, my own existence.
Those years of education also laid a solid base of
historical consciousness, of awareness of the whole
Western historical experience and a methodology for

expanding that awareness that continues to undergird the way I ask and answer questions.

In those days the Scripps education was centered on a twelve-unit-a-year humanities core curriculum. We studied the history, philosophy, literature, art, music, religion, and social thought of each historical period. It was an integrated curriculum, with a team of specialists in different disciplines working together. In this way we studied the first year, not only the Greek and Roman worlds, but also the ancient Near East, the Hebrew Bible and Christian New Testament, and the early Church. The rise of Christianity was situated in its historical framework as a religious movement within the ancient Mediterranean world, as an alien to it, yet ultimately the heir and preserver of its legacy. "Classics," as a part of European education, indeed, exists because a millennium of Christian monks and schoolmen chose to carry along this legacy as a counterpoint in relation to which they shaped Christian theology and culture.

What made me ripe for this kind of intellectual adventure? Even more, what excited an intense critical interest in the contradictions posed by this historical material for my own identity?

On a superficial level my family background would have seemed very different from these concerns. My father was Anglican, Republican, a Virginia gentleman; my mother's paternal line, West Pointers of a traditionalist type. Yet, as I moved from one concern to another, I felt myself very much grounded in a certain basic selfhood that was a legacy of my family.

Ten or twelve years ago I was giving a talk in New York. At the end, a man came up and introduced himself. He turned out to be the son of old family friends whom my parents often visited in my childhood. I knew that he himself had become a psychologist. He said, not critically, but more with a sort of wonder: "It is really surprising that you have become the sort of person you have. Your father was a very conservative man and would have been very much out of sympathy with these ideas." I am not sure what my topic was at that time, but if it was not feminism, it was probably something on Black Liberation or the New Left.

This encounter startled me. It made me reflect on how I could have come such a long way from that very conservative father, while myelf feeling engaged in a natural evolution for myself. Part of the clue to this is undoubtedly that that very conservative father actually had relatively little influence on my personality. My identity was shaped by a much less conservative mother and a community of sisters who worked out our development together after my father's death in 1948 (when I was twelve). He remained for me a shadowy figure, who was away in the Second World War for much of my grade-school years and left again for Greece in 1947. My most intimate memories of him are pleasant but fleeting; trips to the National Geographic films and afterward out for hot fudge sundaes that we shared gleefully, knowing that my mother, with her concerns for too much sugar, would have disdained; a trip to Fotheringay, the old Virginia plantation of his boyhood; a brief few days when I was left alone with him in Greece before his sudden death. Mainly I saw him through the romance of my mother's image of him as the perfect gentlemen. Since I had such little day-to-day contact with him, my few memories are cast in the mold of special holidays.

My own personality I see as much more directly a

product of my mother's influence. She came from an English and Austrian Catholic background, from a family that had a keen sense of roots going back to colonial America, and which had pioneered in California and Mexico. My mother's Catholicism was free-spirited and humanistic. Indeed she gave me the strong impression that the occasionally more narrow-minded statements of priests were simply the expression of badly educated "Irish peasants" and could be safely ignored. While this view may have been as much the product of ethnic bias as intellectual criticism, it certainly never gave me any great fear of disagreeing with clerical authorities!

My mother steered our upbringing in such a way that we tended not much to encounter the more parochial (and ethnic) versions of American Catholicism—a high-toned Jesuit parish which drew theologians from Georgetown University; the friendly private chapel of a nearby Carmelite community; a private rather than a parochial Catholic school; these were the memories of my childhood. The result was that my impression of Catholicism was of something with deep historical roots, both profound and meaningful in content, not something trite or vulgar. Certain obsessions with sex and conduct, which seem to have marred many a Catholic girlhood, thus passed me by. This means that I lack some of the more humorous memories that bind together products of parochial American Catholicism, but I also feel less of the hostility that comes from living down debilitating restrictions on personal and intellectual development.

There was in my mother a romanticism and pride about her family heritage that gave me the sense of inheriting a valuable identity. One got the impression from her that "our people" had been noble and daring adventurers; we came from a heroic past. While much of this seems to have degenerated into a reactionary conservatism, and even racism, in some of my mother's (male) relatives, I was fortunately not much aware of that in my youth. The main impression I got from all this was that my star was solidly set in the firmament of the universe and that anything I decided to do, I could do and do well. This had nothing to do with wealth or power, for my mother herself had been raised by a widow with five children, and she was a widow for much of my childhood. What was distilled out of the situation was a sense of secure self-confidence. This has nothing to do with arrogance—itself an expression of insecurity— but, more a sense of being an equal to anyone in any situation.

Although my mother had her ethnic snobberies, as I have indicated, her childhood in Mexico gave her a deep sympathy for its people, women especially, and the ability to communicate as easily with the wetback working women she often sheltered in her home as with the cultured. The ability to feel at home with all types of people in many walks of life and levels of wealth and poverty was part of what was communicated to me by her sense of humanity. "Peership" with anyone was not with her a form of social-climbing, but a sympathetic outreach to the human condition in its many forms and manifestations. I remember in college, reading a line from the Latin poet Terence, "I am a human, and nothing that is human is alien to me." This line touched a deep, responsive chord in me. I suspect that my mother's personality stood behind something of its immediate resonance.

I also feel lucky that my mother and her generation of

friends were a product of the old feminist movement of
the late nineteenth and early twentieth centuries. Born
in 1895, she went to college in the second decade of our
century and belonged to that era of American women
who saw endless new horizons opening before them.
One of my mother's friends became an artist, another
went to Europe with Jane Addams to work with the
Women's Peace Party (later the Women's International
League for Peace and Freedom). This same friend
worked in interracial community organizing in the
South in the thirties. After my father's death, our family
moved back to my mother's girlhood home in La Jolla,
California. Here she was surrounded until her death in
1978 with the circle of her old friends—almost all
women. These women were an important reference
group for me in my development. Vigorous, intellectually active, and socially concerned into their late
eighties and even nineties, they provided me a sense of
roots for what I was doing. All were keenly interested in
religion. It never occurred to them to think of authentic
religion as something other than the free adventure of
the spirit. In her eighties, my mother had a study circle
of friends who read religious classics from all cultures.

At the funeral Mass for my mother in La Jolla,
California, I insisted on preaching the sermon. Difficult
as it was for me, I felt that the last tribute owed to this
circle of magnificent women was a word that really
reflected the spirit of their lifelong friend, not some
rendition of traditional pieties from a priest who never
knew her. I ended the sermon with these words:

> As she grew older, her tall, straight body shrank and
> bowed, her thick dark curly hair turned gray and then white.

It was as though her physical power was turning more and more into spiritual power. She became almost incandescent as her body became more and more frail and delicate until, at the end, she was like a fine, fragile piece of china, scarcely containing the inner power.

Mother was deeply religious, but in a very individual way, without an element of subservience. It was her daily support.

What perhaps few people knew is how valiantly and stubbornly she fought against the ravages of old age. She refused to become an invalid, even though her arthritis perhaps qualified her to be one twelve or thirteen years ago.

Her diet was always spartan, the heritage of nursing a diabetic mother. In old age her diet became even more strict and vegetarian, with, of course, generous amounts of Mexican *salsa!*

Every morning she took out her exercise pad and rigorously worked on her muscles, trying as much as possible to keep the use of her legs.

She never really accepted the idea that she couldn't walk. Against all odds she insisted on walking, and continued to walk. She loved to hike, to climb the Sierras, to travel down to Mexico, to ramble the California coast. She hated the fact that she could do this less and less.

A few years ago she told me that she had had a dream. She dreamed that she was running, running freely, her legs were strong and lithe again. She was running down the beach, the sea wind blowing in her hair.

It was characteristic of her that when she died, it would not be of a long illness, but suddenly, almost instantaneously, without a cry. Not in a hospital, or even at home, but off on a trip, flying to help a newly widowed daughter. Not in bed, but walking, walking without a cane . . .

Suddenly, without warning, the fragile piece of china broke. Her spirit flies unfettered, running, running down the beach, her legs strong and limber, the sea air blowing in her hair.

And so it shall ever be.

I realize that the reason my own flight into critical freedom and growth always felt so natural, so inevitable,

so firmly supported by the Ground of Being that
upheld me, was because the real heritage upon which I
drew was not the official patriarchal heritage, but the
unofficial matriarchal one. This is the heritage of
mothers and daughters who bond together to maintain
the survival of the human community while the males
are off killing themselves, destroying the world, and
stifling the creative spirit with doctrinaire authoritari-
anism. For me the patriarchal heritage fell away fairly
early, revealing itself to be a façade and a delusion. It is
the matriarchal heritage of mothers and daughters that
underlies my real life. Perhaps this is why I always
instinctively think of God, not as the paternal superego,
but as the empowering matrix.

The Challenge of Classical Humanism

It was as one ripe for intellectual exploration that I
entered college and plunged into what was to become
for me a lifetime of trying to understand and evaluate
the Western cultural and religious experience. Originally I had thought that I wanted to be an artist. Much
of my grade and high school had been spent developing
artistic skills, although my writing abilities also were
honed in two years as editor of the school newspaper.
But in college the verbal seemed to overtake and
submerge the aesthetic direction of my abilities. It was
with words rather than with images that I found I could
better shape my evolving experiences.

In my exploration of the development of Western
culture I was particularly influenced by two brilliant
teachers, Robert Palmer (classicist and translator of
Walter Otto's *Dionysos: Mythos und Kultus*) and Philip
Merlan (a scholar of middle and neo-Platonism). Both
represented the best of that humanistic scholarship

combining both precision and integrative breadth. They were my models of what it means to "learn," not as an alienating task, but as a self-enriching project, a continual expansion of one's own meaning and identity, a taking responsibility for the past in a way that directed one to responsibility for society's present and future.

However, both these men posed very sharp challenges to my inherited Christian faith. Although Palmer came from a German Lutheran background and Merlan from a Viennese Jewish one, both taught very consciously as people who preferred the world-view of Greco-Roman antiquity to that of biblical faith, Jewish or Christian. Both of them inducted us into the classical world, not only as *paideia,* but also as *pietas.* We learned that the stance of the ancient Greek or Roman toward the world was not only one of intellectual questioning or aesthetic appreciation, but also and primarily one of religious awe. I can still remember Philip Merlan describing the idea of the ascent of the soul through the planetary spheres, casting off the psychic influences of each planet at its native star, until, purified and free, it entered the eighth sphere of the fixed stars. With a characteristic gesture, he declared, "I shouldn't be surprised if it happens to me." A classroom of mostly Protestant seminarians gave a slight gasp. It was suddenly evident that we were not just talking about some ancient theory, but describing a real way of situating oneself in the world. One could scarcely understand how such a view shaped the existence of people in the past until one could imagine, at least, for a moment, that it might "happen to me."

The teacher most influential in my interest in religious studies was Robert Palmer. This might appear

paradoxical, because he was also the most outspoken in
his negative evaluation of Christianity. I remember his
saying once that he loved to go to Rome, except that
there were too many Catholics there. I could imagine
him walking in the Roman forum, reconstructing in his
mind's eye the city of Caesar and Cicero. Christian
Rome was for him an unfortunate debasement of the
Eternal City. Christians were a barbarian horde of
squatters who had seized the city, looting the stones of
the ancient temples to build their churches to the
crucified rabbi. Palmer's view of the triumph of
Christianity was rather like that of the fourth-century
rhetor Libanius, who found it incredible that the glory
of classical culture, with its humanism, its balance, it
political culture, could be replaced by a religion that
worshiped dead men's bones and taught people to
scourge their bodies, shun baths and procreation, and,
most of all, to neglect the tasks of civic duty. Once, when
discussing the Emperor Julian's attempt to reinstate
paganism as a mixture of humanism. and neoplatonic
philosophy, Palmer said wistfully: "It had everything.
Why didn't it win?"

Palmer taught me to revere the works of Werner
Jaeger and Walter Otto. From Otto, Palmer took his
favorite formula, "First the god, then the dance, and
finally the story." All religions begin in theophany, the
real encounter with the numinous, present in a
particular way in a particular time and place. "God" in
this sense is plural: "the gods." Although the under-
lying reality of the divine may be one, the appear-
ances of the divine are necessarily many and distinct
according to different configurations of site, community, and historical moment. The gods are no mere
"idols" or human projections, to be unfavorably

contrasted with the one true God of biblical revelation. The god experienced in the oracle of Eleusis was not less real than that which appeared to Moses in the burning bush. The theophany or encounter with the numinous expresses itself first of all in cult; that is to say, in ritual action. The presence of the god is reenacted, made present again, first of all in dance and drama. Only afterward is it formulated as word or story. In that sense theology, the systematizing of the stories, is the stage farthest removed from the actual experience of the god.

This insight was, for me, a valuable aid, not only in taking ancient piety seriously, but also in understanding biblical religion. One cannot start, as I had been taught to do, by asking if you "agree with the doctrine." Rather one must first work back to the story, then to the dance, and finally begin to glimpse the experience that lies behind these expressions. Only then can you begin to understand what the verbal reflection really means. It was from Palmer I discovered that a religious proposition, such as Christ's resurrection, is not primarily a doctrine demanding rational assent to a "fact" about something that happened to someone else long ago, unrelated to myself. Rather it is a statement about something that could "happen to me"; about the renewal of my life. He happened to be talking about the resurrection of Attis, rather than Christ, at the time, but it was a breakthrough experience, an important recognition that religious statements could be existential, rather than merely propositional. The fact that I had to discover this in such a way also says something about the type of religious education I had received in eleven years of Catholic schools.

I had come to Scripps College to study fine arts. It had

not occurred to me that I would become a classics major, much less a theologian. As a result of these challenges I became more and more interested in classical antiquity, and particularly in the puzzle of Christianity's rise and triumph in this world. My B.A. thesis on eschatology in the intertestamental literature, my M.A. in classics and Roman history, and my Ph.D. in classics and patristics would all spring from this continuing interest. In a real sense freshman humanities set the context for questions that I would continue to research for the rest of my life. However, I did not think of this as connected with a career in the church, but with a personal search for the meaning of this history. Indeed, I did not consciously reflect at all on what kind of career this study might be leading to. In the fifties one could still be rather oblivious to economic questions. The anxiety of an unemployed middle class had not yet hit the university. It was still possible to think of oneself as pursuing truth for its own sake. Scripps as a humanities college for women also encouraged this impractical attitude.

Only when I emerged with Ph.D. in hand did it become apparent that one reason for this impracticality was that our male professors never took seriously the idea of our future employability. They assumed we would marry businessmen or scientists and settle down to use our humanistic education to talk wittily at cocktail parties or, at most, to be sponsors of "culture" in the community. Thus they neglected to introduce us to such mundane topics as power, prestige, and promotion in academe. It is only by the sheerest accident that a quest like mine managed to translate into a job. Ten years earlier or fifteen years later, and I suspect it would have been a different story.

Yet this ability to land on one's feet does not quite

make up for the profound sense of betrayal by one's academic mentors I experienced when I realized the deep disparity between the ideals of intellectual excellence they had taught us and their lack of serious-ness about our future. Ultimately this meant that they took our minds seriously, in abstraction from our bodies, but they did not take *us* seriously as women. I did not apply myself to feminist analysis explicitly until 1965, but these experiences were already laying the foundation for it.

Opening the Bible

Given such a background, it might seem rather surprising that I would come to be increasingly interested in biblical religion, even defending "pro-phetic faith" as a better basis than pagan naturalism for such contemporary critical movements as feminism and ecology. My Roman Catholic education was of the prerenewal variety—we studied endlessly the sacra-ments and never opened the Bible. My classical humanist mentors were nothing if not slightly contemp-tuous of biblical religion as cramped and benighted compared with the clear light of Athens. To become interested in the Bible was for them almost a kind of apostasy to the higher achievements of the human spirit. My use of classics as a context for understanding Christianity was very much a personal synthesis, not one intended by them. Indeed, it was a shock to discover that my mentor Palmer, who had studied the classical world in such depth, had only the most cursory knowledge of the church fathers writing in the same periods.

With one of my best friends, a Jewish girl of Orthodox background, I arranged our first course in

Hebrew scripture as an independent study. Gradually I began to integrate work in late Judaism, the intertestamental period, the New Testament, and early Christianity into my studies, drawing on the resources of the Claremont Theological School. There seem to me certain advantages in moving in this way from classical humanism to biblical thought. First of all, it meant that when I read the Bible for the first time I did so with the apparatus of historical-critical thought. After certain initial shocks to my inherited model of Christ, this came to seem the natural way to decipher the Bible. I had relatively little baggage of a precritical biblical schooling to discard. Secondly, it meant that biblical thought, rather than being a drag from an alienating past, could open up to me a world of critical and prophetic vision beyond classical humanism.

I realize that there are many from more traditional Christian or Jewish backgrounds for whom the Bible represents a debilitating obstacle to spiritual freedom. Even to suggest that it might have some significant ideas on any topic, particularly on questions of ecology and feminism, is unthinkable. To speak positively about it is to capitulate to the constricting childhood authority from which they have painfully emancipated themselves. There are others who will receive positive evaluation of biblical ideas with the smug satisfaction of an unshaken religious exclusivism. There is probably no way to keep my ideas on the subject from being misunderstood by people of both camps. Fundamentally I come to the Bible from a different experience.

Although I have come to prefer a biblical world-view to that of classical humanism, I have never identified this with religious exclusivism. Basically I reject exclusivism, whether it be Christian over against Judaism or biblical religion as a whole over against nonbiblical religion. I have gone beyond, but have never forgotten, the theophany of the gods as an authentic manifestation of the divine. My preference for biblical thought is a relative preference for certain lines of religious vision that are characteristically Hebraic, not an absolute preference that rules out true knowledge of God/ess in other places. Nor do I accept the common liberal Christian distinction between particular or historical revelation (higher) and general or natural revelation (lower). All religions are rooted in particular encounters with God/ess and so are in that sense historical, although they may not necessarily make the historical itself a datum of religious experience.

If I feel relatively less betrayed by the biblical world, it is because I happened upon it with a more realistic approach to what it is. I never assumed that it dropped out of heaven undefiled by historical gestation. Rather, I understand it as a product of a human quest for meaning that moved through many different stages and contexts. It is certainly not all of a piece, and it is incomprehensible to me why anyone would expect it to be. It is shaped by, dependent on, and yet responding to, the religious world around it. The world of the psalms and the prophets builds upon the best of ancient Canaanite religion, even as it makes a critical transformation of the Canaanite world-view. Some of the more valuable religious patterns of Hebraic thought are indebted to Near Eastern religion, not only the flood story, but the messianic king, and the prophetic cycle of desolation and re-creation.

That the prophets had something which I have presumed to call an ecological theology has much to do with this inheritance from Canaan. The integration of seasonal time and historical time, nature and society, has behind it the great year cycle of Near Eastern cultic experience. But this legacy takes on another dimension of critical insight only when transformed by that religious genius that, as far as I know, is uniquely Hebraic. It is this genius that transforms the Canaanite year cycle of natural-social renewal into the prophetic dialectic of judgment and promise. The scene of the drama has shifted from seasonal cycles to historical crisis.

There is no way to retreat back to the first world and do justice to the realities of Western society. Western consciousness and action, and increasingly that of the whole world, have been decisively shaped by the Hebraic transformation of seasonal theophanies. This is not a question of nature over against society, but rather nature and society together, the human and nonhuman cosmos as one, appearing differently, depending on whether it is viewed through the theophany of being or the crisis of historical judgment. One might almost see this as the distinction of the aesthetic and the ethical. This does not mean that there is no ethics, personal and social, in the Near Eastern and Greek backgrounds. But this is seen more as the restoration of imminent harmony rather than historical conversion and decision against the dark background of human historical apostasy. Only the Hebraic religious vision has the categories to embrace this second dialectic.

This does not mean that all parts of the canonical Bible rise to the promise of prophetic faith. At its best, prophetic faith represents a decisive break with the pattern of religion that makes the divine a confirming theophany of the existing social order. Instead, the existing social order as a hierarchy of rich over poor, the powerful over the weak, is seen as contrary to God's will, an apostasy to God's intent for creational community. The revelation of God therefore appears as judgment against this apostate order. God comes as advocate of the oppressed, overturner of an unjust order, whose action in history points forward to a reconstructed community that will fulfill God's intent for creation, a time when God's will shall be "done on earth, as it is in heaven." Heaven, in this language, is neither the confirming halo of existing creation, nor is it another world into which we can escape from this world. Rather it is the mandate of that rectified world that stands as judgment and hope over against things as they are.

But even when biblical texts are most clearly in this prophetic mode, not all dimensions of unjust relations may be discerned. The prophet may see clearly the injustice of rich urbanites against impoverished country-folk, or of imperial nations against the small and scattered nation, but may miss entirely the injustice of master-slave relations, of male-female relations in patriarchal, slave-holding society, or else ameliorate these relations in more conventional ways that still take the basic system for granted.

The vision of the world rectified may also degenerate into a vision of world reversal, or "revenge theology," that merely makes of the presently poor and weak new imperial powers triumphing over their former enemies. In significant parts of the Scriptures, both Old and New Testament, the prophetic vision evaporates, allowing God again to become simply the sanctifier of the existing social order, as in much of the law codes and the New Testament household codes. Even at its best, prophetic insight has some limitations of the sociology

of consciousness of its spokesmen (generic not intended). It cannot raise truly critical questions from the
context of those who have not yet gained the voice to
raise such questions, specifically women and slaves.

The prophetic dialectic I believe to be the critical
norm of biblical faith. But it is a norm that existed in
the communities reflected in the texts by constantly
struggling against more conventional ways of understanding religion as a sanctification of existing power
structures or power dreams. It is partial, as all critical
insight is partial, for we can see the dialectic of injustice
and new possibility only from one context, not from all
contexts. It is constantly manifesting itself in new ways
in new contexts. In the Old Testament prophets it arises
first as a way of critiquing naïve nationalism. It also sets
itself against religion and religious elites who use
religion to escape from the questions of justice. "I hate
. . . your solemn assemblies. . . . Take away from me
the noise of your songs; to the melody of your harps I
will not listen," cries the prophet Amos. "But let justice
roll down like waters, and righteousness like an
everflowing stream" (5:21, 23-24).

The biblical critique of religion is valid, I would
contend, primarily as self-critique. When it merely
attacks other people's religion, Canaanite in the Old
Testament, Judaism in the New, it does not speak with
any great insight. It is the genius of the New
Testament that prophetic insight is applied, not only
to self-justifying religion, but also to the temptations
of messianic revenge and, tentatively, to the social
hierarchies of race, sex, and slavery. But these critical
insights are all too quickly lost within the New
Testament church itself in new religious sanctifications
of the Christian status quo. Prophetic critique as the

norm of biblical faith, therefore, is not limited to the insights of the societies that produced the biblical texts. Rather, this principle goes out ahead of us, allowing us to apply it in new ways in new contexts. Only in this way is biblical faith a living faith and not a dead letter.

Reappropriating Catholic Christianity

For some ten years during my undergraduate and graduate education, I attempted to carry on some dialogue about my journey of faith with Catholicism. This was made difficult on two fronts. On the one side, the representatives of official Catholicism available to me at that time tended to be anti-intellectual clerics who looked with suspicion on free questioning. Even the better sort of priests in my parish in La Jolla, California, tended to end by advising me grimly to "pray for faith," often with the hint that I was getting more education than I needed. One summer I took a course in medieval philosophy at the San Diego College for Woman, under the mistaken conception that Catholics would be good at medieval thought. The mindset of the nun who taught this course was very parochial. She took to reprimanding me for reading books without imprimaturs—an idea I found merely humorous. My normal assumption was that an imprimatur was a sign that a book probably was not worth reading. Toward the end of the course she discovered that I was soon to be married. She breathed a sigh of relief and said, "Well, this reading will be of no more danger to you. You will soon be too busy to do any more of it." This statement was profoundly shocking. Apparently she thought that the best way to save my soul was to extinguish my mind in a diaper pail. Such a statement was a profound apostasy from her vocation as a woman educator of women.

Yet my mentors at Scripps College were not much more helpful. If my classical professors could barely imagine why one would be interested in the Bible, the professors of second year humanities, covering the medieval and reformation worlds, were scarcely more sympathetic to the Catholic tradition. Our history professor for this period was a grim New England Calvinist who regarded the entire Middle Ages as something fortunately abolished by the Reformation. Monasticism was seen primarily through the lens of its rejection by Protestantism, as inhuman denial of community and at the same time a cover for secret vice. Luther's criticism of "good works" was deformed into a mere fiat against "Catholic ritualism."

Much useful critical material for my evaluation of Catholicism came from this year. For example, I was shocked to learn that the church condoned slavery and serfdom, and was one of the last to give up serfs itself. This certainly set my mind working about the credibility of the church as a moral teacher. But I was also outraged by the self-righteous bigotry with which this whole era of Christianity was treated. There was a kind of implicit triumphalism in these Protestant professors. They assumed that once Catholics such as myself became "enlightened," we would have no logical choice except to leave Catholicism. Catholicism was seen as a relic of a moribund past, already superseded, having no further right to exist. This aroused ethnocentric proclivities that I did not previously know I had. I became determined that, however "enlightened" I became, I would never express it by joining any of "their" churches.

I set out to find the deeper and more intellectually challenging heritage of Catholicism that I knew was surely there. I felt we had been sold short by these professors. They were incapable of opening up the more creative, profound, and also rambunctious, side of the medieval world. While our classical professors taught us antiquity as ones who loved that world and drew us into it as a heritage to own, our professors of the Middle Ages taught us the period through eyes narrowed with hatred and rejection. They saw a world that had to be refuted in order to justify the Reformation. I still feel handicapped by never having studied the Middle Ages with a genuine medievalist.

My annoyance at Protestant triumphalism did not prevent me from exploring a variety of Christian traditions. My graduate studies took me through Reformation and modern Protestant theology. I found Luther and Barth very helpful in critiquing institutional self-idolatry. But there remained something in the Augustinian dualism of nature and grace that was foreign to my spirit. My doctoral studies also opened up the world of Eastern Orthodoxy. In spite of the stasis of its historical development, I still suspect that the Orthodox tradition has the most authentic vision of the union of nature and grace, self and cosmos, one that has tended to get lost in the quasi-Marcionism of Western theology.

Most of mother's friends in La Jolla had become Quakers, and I found much delightful company with them. My father's Anglicanism had never much attracted me. But in college, I began to discover a different breed of Episcopal social activists who made the liturgy a place for new awareness of peace and civil rights issues. Gradually I began to shape a different Catholic identity that might be more properly called ecumenical Christianity.

It seems to me that Christianity is a very complex synthesis of themes. Far from being "simple and pure" in origin, it is the most eclectic of religions, gathering up the whole complex of heritages of the ancient world into a new synthesis. This is its wealth and the source of continual redevelopment. But this complex of themes can never be put together in one final formula. There remains a variety of different emphases, each of which must be affirmed as an aspect of the whole message. The "speciality" of one tradition tends to be neglected in the other traditions. This is why one needs to affirm the whole array of Christian traditions, East and West, Protestant and Catholic, magisterial and radical reformations.

Catholicism exists only in a rich dialogue between these historical communities. Nor am I interested in collapsing these heritages into one big corporation merger, the institutional version of ecumenism. I see the solution to the ecumenical question as communion between traditions, not amalgamation or institutional merger into the lowest common denominator.

In this pluralism of traditions, each Christian church stands in some particularity or another, as well as in dialogue with the whole. They find in that particularity several things. First they are able to appropriate, hopefully, the particular genius of that tradition as something meaningful to themselves. Secondly, they learn to accept their own particular ethnic family, not as the best, but simply as their own, the one they know and therefore the one they can rightfully criticize in love rather than rebellion. Finally, they know that each of these communities is, in its own way, apostate to the Lord, to the messianic humanity. The communities exist, not as the elect, or the righteous ones, but as forgiven sinners, as ones who affirm their origins and future hope in Christ as a gift to be received again and again, despite their failures. In this sense all our particular heritages have to be continually renewed (not forgotten) in critical encounter with the prophetic word. No tradition, by reason of its size or longevity, is automatically nearer or farther from that prophetic word, which is our real foundation. In this sense, all talk of historical foundations, apostolic succession, and validity of orders is institutional reification with no relevance to Christian authenticity.

In my reappropriation of the Roman Catholic community, not as the best, the oldest, or even the widest, base for ecumenism, but simply as my part of the apostate church that needed to enter into dialogue with the others and with the Christ, I was greatly helped by the whole set of new developments that began to take place in this community in the sixties. The Second Vatican Council and its after-effects began to blow open the closed Catholic world. All the doubts and questions that many Catholics had felt, but had not believed they should tell others, or even admit privately, began to get communicated with increasing freedom.

During this period my husband and I belonged to a creative community associated with the Benedictine priory of St. Andrews in Valyermo, California. The monks of Valyermo were originally from Belgium and had come to California by way of a twenty-year sojourn in China. Expelled by the Communist revolution, they settled in the high desert area of Southern California. Their life-style blended the Zen Buddhist sense of simplicity and harmony with nature with renewed Benedictinism.

Here was a Catholic Christianity with conscious roots

far older than the counter-Reformation Catholicism
that had shaped what was known as the Roman Catholic
Church. The Benedictine life-style was created in
response to the collapse of civilization of late antiquity.
But this consciousness of tradition also made them open
and flexible toward contemporary questions. Understanding the relativity of cultures, they did not
absolutize a fairly recent and parochial world-view as
unchangeable. Their simplicity of life was completely
devoid of masochism. The ideal I glimpsed there was
one of simplicity and peace that was at the same time
wholesome and vitalizing.

Father Vincent Martin, perhaps the leading intellectual of the community, once described Benedictine life
as a dance, not a frenzied dance, but an orderly and
seemingly effortless round of work, prayer, and study,
of silence and conversation, of seasons of joy and
seasons of sorrow. This was the bulwark of humanized
life built in the fifth century against the background of a
disintegrating civilization, one which may yet provide
new answers in a new time of disintegration. As a total
answer monasticism seemed to me inadequate. I did not
forget Palmer's questions about Christianity as the
deserters of the tasks of civic responsibility. But as a
resource in the larger rhythm of existence, it could
provide a dimension missing in modern life.

The great mistake of Christian monasticism as it
originally developed, was in defining itself as a
community of celibates with lifelong vows and voca-
tions, an elite set apart from the rest of the church. So it
missed the opportunity to be seen as a stage of life, as in
Asian monasticism, or as a resource where those in
active life could retire for periodic renewal of energies
and vision. This was actually the way such monastic

communities as Valyermo were being used. But the tradition of permanent vows obscured the more consistent development of this option. Nevertheless, I greatly value my time as a "temporary monk." I wrote much of my Ph.D. thesis on Gregory of Naziansus as rhetor and philosopher (monk) in the rose-covered cottage at Valyermo. I can still vividly remember rising before dawn to walk the desert hills at sunrise, and then, at the sound of the distant bell, walking down amid sweetly smelling sage to Matins.

During this period of the late sixties, dialogue with many other Catholic thinkers opened up for me. There was the correspondence and lasting friendship with people such as Thomas Merton and Gregory Baum. The newly militant Catholic antiwar movement began to produce resistance communities around figures such as the Berrigan brothers. I became involved in the Harrisburg Defense group to defeat the FBI's trumped-up conspiracy charges against Philip Berrigan and Elizabeth McAlister, although I was never entirely sympathetic with the personalist heroics of this branch of the movement. My closest ties were with the Washington-based Community for Creative Non-Violence, begun by Paulist Father Ed Guinan. This community, which combined peace activism with the traditional Catholic worker activities like soup kitchens and medical and legal defense for the poor, seemed to have the right combination of persistence and good humor to save it from the sectarian styles of self-righteousness.

Like a giant emerging from a drugged sleep, the Catholic world seems to be testing its new-found consciousness in every direction. In theology, in social action, and in the building of intentional communities, some of the most exciting activity on the Christian scene was coming from this community. The development of liberation theology in Latin America, Catholic feminism, the Base Community movement in both Europe and the Third World, provided expanding and international communities of Catholics to which I felt a special affinity.

All the ideas and questions that I had been developing in fifteen years of journeying into Christian origins and history found their place in these new Catholic renewal communities who were hungry for just such critical resources. My own individual history, in this sense, joined with the history of Catholic renewal and became a part of it. The questioning of hierarchical authority and its self-justifications was not lessened thereby, but indeed has increased and become far more critical. This questioning now finds its echo in a vast community of people who communicate through the same media and share a critical culture, rather than in isolated individuals. It has become a part of a dialectic of renewal within historic Catholicism itself, whose outcome is still uncertain, but which can no longer be disenfranchised.

2
The Question of Jewish-Christian Relations

Unmasking the Myth of
the Judaeo-Christian Tradition

I am asked by Jews about my enduring interest in the question of anti-Semitism in Christian theology. This is a sensitivity that Jews do not ordinarily expect Christians to possess. When a Christian displays a particular concern for this issue, Jews tend to assume that there is some personal element in one's biography that explains this, most likely some Jewish ancestry. Indeed many of the Christians who have been involved in Jewish-Christian dialogue were themselves either converted Jews or had Jewish parentage. Since in some of my writings on the subject I have mentioned my Jewish uncle, it is assumed that I likewise have this kind of personal concern based in my family identity.

As it happens, this is not exactly the case. My uncle David was not a blood relative, but the husband of my father's sister. Like many American Jews growing up in the 1920s, he identified with a "universal" Western cultural tradition and buried his own Jewish identity. He was important to me and my sisters in introducing us to the classics of Western music and art. He sang in a fine tenor of operatic quality and taught us to love Mozart and Rembrandt. But he never spoke to us of Judaism. His own Jewish family in New York City remained a kind of secret. I met them only when I became the executor for my aunt's estate after both their deaths. I heard from my mother that he flirted all his life with Catholicism, was almost converted by Bishop Fulton Sheen, but never took the final step. His Jewishness was buried in the unspoken agony of an unresolved personal identity.

His marriage to my aunt Sophie Radford was something of an anomaly. A feminine woman of Southern Anglican gentry, she was fond of him without, I think, being able in any way to understand his interests or conflicts. She served unconsciously to ratify his escape from his background. A man of great talent, my uncle seemed peculiarly unable to fulfill his own potential. He hid his light under a bushel in a middle-level job and expressed his artistic loves in the private world of his home and family. In middle age he declined into rapid senility, as though infected with a secret urge to suicide that he could express only passively (his father had committed suicide). Thus my uncle did not actively direct my attention to Judaism. It is only much later, in the light of an interest awakened from other sources, that some of his cultural roots came into focus.

Yet it does seem to me that I have had a latent sensitivity to this issue for a long time. When I was a child I remember feeling an instinctive protest against anti-Semitic remarks casually dropped from the lips of Christians. I was nine at the end of world War II. In those days newsreels were still shown in movie houses. In between the Saturday cat-and-mouse cartoons, I remember being exposed to pure horror. The films of the emaciated skeletons of the death-camp survivors flashed across the screen in my neighborhood theater. The story of Anne Frank also made a large impression upon me.

Our Western civilization course at Scripps College managed almost entirely to ignore Jewish history in the Christian era. It was not until my sophomore year that I even heard the word "pogrom" from a Jewish fellow student, and then had to inquire naïvely what it meant. Yet I remember feeling an electric rush of emotion when a teacher casually mentioned that the Jews had been in exile from the failure of the Jewish wars at the beginning of the Christian era until the founding of the state of Israel in 1945. Whenever the subject of the Jews was mentioned, I seemed to feel a special pang of personal pathos, as though here was a mystery that must be explored, a secret that underlay some unspoken tragedy of our whole civilization. It is possible that my uncle helped to create that sensitivity in an unintended way.

My awareness of the "Jewish question" in Christian theology was developed by the somewhat circuitous route of reading in Christian origins. As an undergraduate I became curious to understand the development of the concept of afterlife in early Christianity. I worked this through in a B.A. thesis on the development of eschatology in the intertestamental Jewish apocalyptic literature (1958). In the process of doing this, I became aware of several important themes that have continued to concern me ever since. First of all, I discovered that what Judaism meant by the word "Messiah" at the time of Jesus had very little in common with what the Catholic tradition taught as the meaning of the word "Christ." Christ was understood as a divine man, the incarnation of the Word of God who appeared to save us from personal sin, reconcile us with God, and make immortal life available to the redeemed.

The Messiah, on the other hand, was not an incarnate divinity, but a human king and warrior who represented God. His deeds were not focused primarily on the personal realm of sin and life after death. Rather he was a historical actor who appeared at the end of the era of injustice, to defeat real physical enemies of Israel, to end oppression, and to inaugurate a new era of peace and justice. In the apocalyptic writings, the Messiah belongs to the temporal era of the millennium. He has nothing to do with saving us from mortality or making available life after death.

As a child in Catholic schools I had always been told that the Jews were waiting for long centuries in "darkness" for the coming of the Messiah. Then Jesus arrived and fulfilled their expectations. But, for some unexplained reason—usually described as due to generic "stubbornness"—they refused to accept him. It was taken for granted that Jesus was exactly what the Jews were waiting for—or, at least, what they *ought* to have been waiting for, if they had understood their own prophets and scriptures rightly. But the Jews also had the "wrong idea" about the Messiah, a nationalist and materialist idea, which prevented them from recognizing Jesus as the true fulfillment of their own hopes.

Having read the Jewish literature of messianic hope, the apocalyptic writings from the second century B.C. to the end of the first century A.D., I came to see these kinds of Christan assumptions in a radically different light. A large gap opened up between the Jewish idea of the Messiah and the Catholic idea of Christ. In between the two stood the figure of the historical Jesus, remote from the idea of the Messiah, but equally remote from the Christian idea of the Christ. If Jesus never claimed to be a warrior and king who would end historical injustice by leading the forces of God at Armageddon, it was also apparent that he never claimed to be an incarnate divinity, to bestow immortality, or even to found a Christian church as a separate religion from Judaism.

It seemed to me very problematic to fault the Jews for not accepting Jesus as the Christ, when what their tradition meant by the Messiah had nothing to do with this Christian concept of the Christ. But, if one did not fault the Jews for their nonacceptance, then the whole Christian claim to inherit the religion of fulfilled Jewish messianic hope was thrown into question. The connecting thread linking Jewish messianic expectation, Jesus' historical life and acts, and Christianity was broken. They lay, like so many disparate pieces, tendentiously tied together by later Christian myth-making.

It was also peculiar that none of my teachers on Christian origins seemed aware of this contradiction. Nor did the scholarship satisfactorily address this issue. Scholars might succeed, by recondite and elaborate argumentation, to link up two of these terms somewhat, but never all three. They might succeed in showing that Jesus was related at least to some of the ideas that circulated in Judaism under messianic hope, such as proclaiming sight to the blind and release to the captive—although they always seemed to finesse the fact that he did not do these things on a sociopolitical plane, which was, in fact, the plane on which the Messiah was supposed to act. Or they might, by equally circuitous reasoning, link up some aspects of the picture of Jesus with later Christology. But the connection between all three always broke down decisively at some point.

The authors generally fell into accusing one or another of the end poles of this relation of some kind of apostasy. Either Catholic Christianity was accused of having sold out the true idea of Christ taught by Jesus, or the Jews were accused of having failed to understand the true idea of Christ. Yet the authors seem unaware that if one or another of these poles collapsed, the traditional myth of Christianity as the fulfillment of Jewish messianic hope could not be maintained. If the historical concept of Christ was not what Jesus taught, then the legitimacy of Christianity was undermined at its origins.

If, on the other hand, the concept of Christ, legitimately developed by the church out of the teaching of Jesus, had no continuity with Jewish messianic hope, then Christianity could not claim to fulfill Jewish messianic hope. One could not, simultaneously, claim to fulfill a Jewish messianic idea and also repudiate that same idea as wrong. *Whose idea was the Messiah anyway, if not the Jews'?* If Christianity has the true idea of Christ, surely that idea has to be found somewhere in the Jewish tradition. If it is nowhere to be found in their tradition, then the Christian idea of Christ is not, in fact, a fulfillment of the Jewish idea of the Messiah. Rather, it is a quite different construct of ideas that accidentally got attached to Christian claims of Jewish biblical legitimacy, but whose actual historical origins derive from another set of cultural traditions.

The logic of this dilemma seemed to me inescapable. Yet it was surprising how it constantly managed to escape the learned professors. It was almost as though the whole enterprise of Christian scholarship concerning its own origins was intended to mystify and cover up, rather than to identify and clarify this basic problem of Christian legitimacy *vis à vis* Jewish messianic hope.

Lacking any satisfactory treatment of this subject, I set to putting together some pieces of it for myself. In the late sixties I began writing on the Messiah of Israel and the Cosmic Christ. I undertook to describe the roots of the Jewish messianic idea in Near Eastern kingship and New Year rituals. I traced the evolution of the messianic idea into its apocalyptic form, and I tried to situate Jesus in the context of first-century Jewish messianism. Then I traced a second set of ideas about the primordial Mind and paradigmatic "Man" who represented the form and essence of creation. These became a separate soteriological myth unconnected originally with messianic ideas. Christian Christology is revealed as a gradual elimination of the Jewish messianic concepts and a substitution of these cosmic soteriological ideas, although retaining the confusing title of the Christ (Messiah) for this divine savior.

I went on to demonstrate how, in the fourth century, in the definition of classical Christology, many of the contradictions of this composite tradition came to a head. A Constantinian imperial Christ competed with a

Donatist anti-imperial apocalyptic Christ. A private, other-worldly soteriology conflicted with a repoliticized Christ who was used to ratify an established Christian imperial power. Even the divine mother of the ancient Near Eastern myth of the dying and rising savior got smuggled in again as Mary, the Mother of Jesus.

The family tree of these ideas can be identified, but many of the crucial stages came about through "illegitimate" marriages. The Canaanite origin of Jewish ideas and the eclectic origin of Christian ideas become suppressed family secrets. Scholarship labors to substitute legitimate for illegitimate parentage at each crucial point in the legacy. Since my own classical training had dissuaded me of these prejudices and given me every reason to assume that a Canaanite idea might be as legitimate as a Jewish one, a pagan idea as legitimate as a Christian one, the scholarly enterprise seemed to create hopeless obscurantism and prevent an accurate understanding of where our ideas have actually come from and what they meant (and might mean). One cannot correctly pose the question of the meaning of Christian identity today until one is willing to tell the story of Christian origins truthfully. Or, to put it another way, people who have to lie about their history cannot clarify their identity.

This seemed to me a fundamental principle and purpose of historical research. At one point it occurred to me that a search for a truthful account of one's history was the collective analogue to psychoanalysis. The resolution of neurotic habits in the present is related to the discovery and acceptance of a true account of one's past. Just as individuals have neuroses that are linked to cover-ups about their past, so historical groups also have neuroses linked with cover-ups in their past.

The twin pathologies of Christianity toward both paganism and Judaism are related to its long historical misrepresentation of its true relationship to these two cultures of antiquity.

In 1970 I finished this laborious manuscript of some 460 pages and sent it to Oxford University Press (which had published my Ph.D. thesis on Gregory Nazianzus). It was scornfully rejected on the critique of a scholar who was clearly hostile to the section on Canaanite origins of messianic ideas. It became clear to me that much more work still needed to be done in polishing the details, but it also has stood the test of my last ten years of research as a basically accurate account.

This manuscript has also been the source of many offspring. The link of the Canaanite Anath at the beginning of my account and the Christian Mary at the end now becomes a whole arena for feminist critique. The anti-Judaic question was implicit in this research, but was not developed. The issues of feminism and anti-Semitism have become spin-off areas of writing where I have drawn upon the whole vast background opened up through this exploration. But the original manuscript still lies in my drawer unpublished, although I constantly use pieces of it in teaching and writing. I am not sure whether I will ever go back and do the polishing necessary to publish this work, yet it lies behind much of my subsequent writing on Christian origins in Christology, anti-Semitism, the Goddess and Mariology, and, finally, on political theology. In the rest of this section I would like to discuss particularly the two areas of Christology and anti-Semitism.

Shortly after I finished the writing on Christology, I began some research on patristic views of women. I was involved in editing a volume on the Jewish and

Christian attitudes, subsequently published as *Religion and Sexism: Images and Women in the Jewish and Christian Tradition* (Simon & Schuster, 1974). As I explored attitudes toward women in the church fathers, I also noted their disparaging views of the Jews. I became aware of a curious parallelism. The basic model in patristic thought for relating to the "other" was in terms of head to body, spirit to flesh. Flesh was treated both as inferior and as morally subversive to the higher demands of the spirit. Jews and Judaism were located in relationship to Christianity along the lines of this dualism in two different ways. First, the revelation of the "old covenant" was described as a "fleshly foreshadowing" of what has been fulfilled in Christianity on a higher and spiritual plane. Secondly, contemporary Jews and Judaism were regarded as possessing a carnal and materialistic religion that lacked true spirituality. This was used as an explanation for the post-Christian inferiority of Judaism and its inability to accept its own transcendence in Christianity.

My research precipitated a new determination to follow systematically the question of anti-Semitism in Christian theology, to show its origins in the conflict of Judaism and early Christianity over the messianic idea, its development in the church fathers, and its subsequent course in the Christian tradition up to the present. Although the work would focus primarily on the patristic material and its background in New Testament Christianity, one could not avoid recognizing some contemporary links with the virulent anti-Semitism that led to the Holocaust. I began this research in the spring of 1971 and completed it while I was a visiting lecturer at Harvard Divinity School, 1971–72 (*Faith and Fratricide*, The Seabury Press, 1974).

I had been invited to Harvard as a feminist and liberation theologian, a type that Harvard was glad to patronize as visitors, but never to embrace as a member of their "club." I had been teaching at Howard University since 1965 and had been concerned more with political and black theology than with feminist theology. The year at Harvard offered me a chance to work through questions of feminism systematically, both in Christian origins and contemporary culture. In doing so, I came to realize how faddish "social" theologies are apt to be. I had as part of my constituency some radical feminists of the Harvard Divinity School student body. As a feminist theologian I was regarded as the "coming thing," riding the new wave of critical thought. But the fact that I was equally concerned with racism and poverty was regarded in a slightly pitying manner, as though I was "still back in the sixties." To be concerned about class and race was seen as distracting from "pure" feminism. The influence of Mary Daly was evident here.

But, most of all, the fact that I was teaching a course and writing a book on patristic anti-Semitism was seen by these feminists as a puzzling anomaly that did not fit any of their expectations. Anti-Semitism was not even a fad become passé for them. It simply did not make any sense at all. Feminists presumably should see Judaism as the granddaddy of patriarchal misogyny. Liberation theologians should sympathize with the Third World, not with Jews. These things were never said in so many words, but they were conveyed by the uncomprehending expressions that I got when I shared with the students material from my researches. Probably my most sympathetic hearing that year was from some feminist Jewish women. They began to reexamine their repudiation of their synagogue backgrounds and their ready identification of Harvard Divinity School culture with "universalism." The hidden negative messages about Judaism in Christian theology began to become audible to them for the first time.

This experience alerted me to the ambivalent relationship between personal search and the public popularity of ideas. Part of my own success in teaching, publishing, and lecturing comes from a congruence between my own personal concerns and the concerns of a progressive sector of the churches and the society. But if I have had, or can continue to have, anything really significant to say, I cannot afford to take my cues from what is *au courant*. I have to work primarily out of a sense of my personal integrity. The content of cultural critique cannot be the current mood of the year or the decade, but must be a systematic exploration of the pathologies and redeeming graces of the Christian tradition over its whole history, in its many branches, and in its implications for worldwide culture today and in the future. Only then do these various concerns with sexism, racism, political and liberation theologies, and anti-Semitism hang together as a critique of the pathologies of the tradition and a search for its reconstruction. Otherwise they remain passing and disconnected "fads."

Raising the question of the Christian roots of anti-Semitism and its implications for theology was a quest consonant with my sense of the total problem of Christian history. But it was also dissonant with popular American "left" culture in 1972. Even today, the book that came out of that research remains better known in German translation in Europe than in America, and better known among American Jews than among Christians. When I went to publish the book, I encountered very odd responses. One reputable secular publisher with a large religious listing seemed to lose the book for a while. It finally showed up in the mail in a battered condition and without an accompanying letter. Later they wrote that they regarded the book as too "heavy" and wanted to know whether I might recast it in a more popular, novelistic form "like Morton's, *Secret Gospel*"!

A university publisher told me it was not scholarly enough, and they might consider it if I would delete the last chapter on theological reconstruction and leave only the historical account. Finally, a religious house agreed to take it, but without advance royalties since, in their words, "'Christians don't like to read about anti-Semitism." The implication was that the book would never sell. I felt somewhat vindicated when the book won a top-ten in the National Book Awards for Religion. But it is evident that I had touched a neurotic nerve in Christians, including those who have been prominent on the Jewish-Christian dialogue circuit.

Many such Christians have developed a mode of ecumenism with Jews that does not force them to reexamine the roots of their faith. They have attributed anti-Semitism to more extraneous cultural factors. Their Jewish counterparts have not pressed them to go farther, partly, I suppose, because they did not feel empowered to challenge Christian theology. But also, I suspect, because they feared to awaken what they, from long experience, recognized to be a pathology that readily turned to violence on subjects such as Christology and messianism. Better to let sleeping dragons lie.

I have encountered very different responses to this work from Jews and from Christians. For Jews the critique is not surprising. It corresponds, to a large extent, with what they already know. But they are astonished that a Christian can say it, and, more so, that such a person remains a Christian. From Christians (with a few notable exceptions) I encounter incomprehension. First, the long history of Christian bigotry and violence toward Jews is unknown to them. They find it hard to believe that they could have studied history and have not been told about this. Second, they become openly hostile and fall into personal attacks when the link between Christology and anti-Semitism is raised. They find it unthinkable that there could be any connection between the two. Often, in the process of reaffirming their understanding of Christology, they verbally reiterate exactly the sort of anti-Judaic patterns of Christian thought which I have described as the "left hand of Christology!"

Such experiences reinforce my impression that anti-Judaic patterns in Christian thought are very deep, woven into the fabric of Christian thought, as much unconscious as conscious, and not dependent on the existence of contemporary sociological friction with existing Jewish communities. This is discouraging, because it also suggests the near impossibility of eradicating these patterns. At most, perhaps, they can be modified sufficiently, while, at the same time, building solidarity with the Jewish community to prevent their being translated into new pogroms.

Christology and Anti-Judaism:
Reconstruction of the Tradition

The anti-Semitic heritage of Christian civilization is neither an accidental nor a peripheral element. It cannot be dismissed as a legacy from paganism or as a product of purely sociological conflicts between the church and the synagogue. Anti-Semitism in Western civilization springs, at its root, from Christian theological anti-Judaism. It was Christian theology that developed the thesis of the reprobate status of the Jew in history and laid the foundations for the demonic view of the Jew that fanned the flames of popular hatred. This hatred was not only inculcated by Christian preaching and exegesis. It became incorporated into the structure of canon law and also into the civil law formed under the Christian Roman emperors, such as the codes of Theodosius (A.D. 428) and of Justinian (6th century). These anti-Judaic laws of the church and the Christian empire laid the basis in Christian society for the debasement of the civic and personal status of the Jew, which lasted until the emancipation in the nineteenth century. These laws were, in part, revived in the Nazi Nuremberg laws of 1933.

The understanding of Christology is, I believe, at the heart of the problem. Theologically, anti-Judaism developed as the left hand of Christology. Anti-Judaism was the negative side of the Christian affirmation that Jesus was the Christ. Christianity claimed that the Jewish tradition of messianic hope was fulfilled in Jesus. But since the Jewish religious teachers rejected this claim, the church developed a polemic against the Jews and Judaism to explain how the church could claim to be the fulfillment of a Jewish religious tradition when the Jewish religious teachers themselves denied it.

At the root of this dispute lies a fundamentally different understanding of the messianic idea that developed in Christianity, in contrast to the Hebrew scriptures and the Jewish teaching tradition. Judaism looked to the messianic coming as a public, world-historical event which would unequivocally overthrow the forces of evil in the world and establish the Reign of God. Originally Christianity also understood Jesus' messianic role in terms of an imminent occurrence of this coming Reign of God. But when this event failed to materialize, Christianity pushed it off into an indefinite future, i.e., the Second Coming, and reinterpreted Jesus' messianic role as inward and personal with little resemblance to what Jewish tradition meant by the coming of the Messiah. An impasse developed between Christianity and Judaism, rooted in Christian claims to messianic fulfillment and supersession of Judaism that were not only unacceptable, but incomprehensible, in the Jewish tradition. The real difference between these views has never really been discussed between Christians and Jews in any genuine fashion because, at an early stage of development, these growing differences of understanding of the messianic advent were covered over with communal alienation and mutual polemic.

Christian teachers sought to vindicate their belief in Jesus as the Christ by reinterpreting Hebrew prophecy to accord with the Christian view of Christ. This Christian exegesis also denied the ability of the Jewish teachers to interpret their own scriptures. The Jews, Christians said, had always been apostate from God and their teachers spiritually blind and hard of heart. In effect, Christian theology set out to demonstrate the rejected status of the Jewish people and the spiritual blindness of its exegesis and piety in order to vindicate the correctness of its own exegesis and its claim to be the rightful heir of Israel's election.

According to Christian teaching, it is the church that is the true heir to the promises to Abraham. It is the spiritual and universal Israel, foretold by the prophets, while the Jews are the heirs of an evil history of perfidy, apostasy, and murder. As a result the Jewish people have been cut off from their divine election. Divine wrath has been poured down on them in the destruction of the temple and the national capital city of Jerusalem. They have been driven into exile and will be under a divine curse as wanderers and reprobates until the end of history, when Jesus returns as the Christ, and the Jews finally have to acknowledge their error.

In effect, the church set up its polemic against the Jews as a historical task of Christians to maintain perpetually the despised status of the Jews as a proof of their divine reprobation. At the same time, the church taught that the Jews must be preserved to the end of history as "witness" to the ultimate triumph of the church. This theological stance was expressed in the official policy of the church toward the Jews through the centuries, combining social denigration with pressure for conversion. It also unleashed waves of hatred and violence that were seldom controllable within the official church policy of minimal protection of Jewish survival. In nazism the Christian demonization of the Jew's spiritual condition was converted into a demonization of their biological condition. Hence the Nazi final solution to the Jewish question was not religious conversion, but physical extermination, to make way for the millennium of the Third Reich.

For us, who live after the Holocaust, after the collapse of Christian eschatology into nazi genocidal destruction, profound reassessment of this whole heritage becomes necessary. Although the Nazis hated Christians as well as Jews, the church nevertheless must take responsibility for the perpetuation of the demonic myth of the Jew that allowed the Nazis to make them the scapegoat of their project of racial purity. This

Christian tradition also promoted an antipathy toward Jews, which generated little need to respond to the disappearance of their Jewish neighbors. We have to examine the roots of the theological patterns that fed this attitude toward the Jews and perpetuate it, even in liberal theologies, today.

Let us consider three basic theological patterns that promote anti-Judaism and see how these dualistic patterns of Christian faith and the negation of Judaism have operated historically. I will present critical reconstructions of these theses, hopefully freed from their anti-Jewish bias, and will focus on Christology as the center around which these dualisms cluster, and ask how Christology itself has to be reconstructed in the light of these criticisms.

The Schism of Judgment and Promise

The Christian *Adversus Judaeos* tradition was built on a two-sided exegesis of the Hebrew scriptures. On the one hand, Christian *midrash* of the psalms and prophets sought to show that the scriptures predicted Jesus as the Christ, and also that they demonstrated the perfidy of the Jews and predicted their final apostasy. This exegesis was developed by Christian teachers before the New Testament was written as a part of the oral tradition of catechetics. It was incorporated into the exegesis and theology of the New Testament. The argument continued as a proof-texting tradition into the patristic period. Writings against the Jews in the corpus of the church fathers continued to be built on a tradition of christological and anti-Judaic prooftexts. This exegetical tradition shows the close connection between Christology and anti-Judaism.

This type of exegesis distorted fundamentally the

meaning of prophetic criticism. The dialectical structure of prophetic thought was split apart, so that its affirmative side, of forgiveness and promise, was assigned to the Christian church, while its negative side, of divine wrath and rejection, was read out against the Jews. This splitting of the left hand of prophetic criticism from the right hand of hope and promise creates an unrelieved caricature of evil, projected upon another people with whom the Christian no longer identifies. The church thereby divorces herself from the heritage of prophetic self-criticism and stands triumphant and perfect. The Hebrew scriptures, which actually contain the tradition of Jewish religious self-criticism and repentance, is turned into a remorseless denunciation. All the evils condemned by the prophets are seen as characteristic of this perfidious people. Anti-Judaism and ecclesiastical triumphalism arise as two distortions of a false polarization of the prophetic dialectic.

This ancient Christian tradition of exegesis has practically disappeared among Old Testament scholars. Most Christian scholars of Hebrew scripture interpret them historically, and not as predictions of Jesus as Christ. This leaves largely unexplained the theological claim that the New Testament "fulfills" the Old (the term "Old Testament" itself, of course, reflects a christological and anti-Judaic bias).

A more difficult problem occurs in the New Testament. Here anti-Judaic exegesis has been woven into the very patterns of theological interpretation and put into the mouth of Jesus himself. Consider, for example, denunciations of the scribes and Pharisees that occur in the Synoptic Gospels. I suggest that we have here two stages of development. In the first stage, in the ministry of Jesus, there is a denunciation of hypocritical religion that stands in the authentic line of Hebrew prophecy.

As the prophet Amos cried out against externalized ritual: "I hate, I despise your feasts, and I take no delight in your solemn assemblies . . . take away from me the noise of your songs, to the melody of your harps I will not listen, but let justice roll down like waters and righteousness like an ever flowing stream" (5:21, 23-24). So the Jesus of the Synoptics cries out: "Woe to you, scribes and Pharisees, hypocrites! for you tithe mint and cummin and have neglected the weightier matters of the law, justice and mercy and faith; these you ought to have done without neglecting the others" (Matt. 23:23).

Such denunciations are not rejections of Judaism, but are built upon Judaism itself. They presuppose Hebrew faith and existence within the covenant of Israel. The Matthew passage does not in any way reject the Torah. It stands within the debate of rabbinic schools of Jesus' time about the priorities for interpreting and following Torah.

A second stage occurs when the Christian church comes to perceive itself as a fundamentally new covenant founded on the new way of salvation, Christ, that supersedes the Torah and renders it obsolete and inferior. Then the prophetic critique of hypocritical ways of living the Law come to be read as a denunciation of the Law itself as *essentially* hypocritical. The criticism of bad scribes and Pharisees is taken to be a rejection of all Jewish scribes and Pharisees as essentially teachers of this bad religion rejected by Jesus.

The shift from one to the other may appear subtle, but, in fact, it is fundamental. In contemporary terms, it would be the difference between the person who denounces a patriarchal reading of Christology and the person who denounces Christology as essentially patriarchal and calls on all people who desire justice to leave the Christian church and found a new religion based on a different soteriological principle. The first person remains within the Christian tradition, though what is said to many may be unacceptable. The second person rejects the Christian community as a context of identity.

The Jesus who announced a coming Reign of God and preached to the poor in a manner critical of religious elites was undoubtedly a radical and controversial figure, but not one who stood in any way outside the Jewish tradition. Contemporary Jewish scholars have no difficulty affirming this Jesus as a part of the spectrum of controversy over the Law and the Kingdom in the first century. But the Christ of Christian faith, whose messianic identity has been translated into a supersessionary principle over against the Torah, is a figure that departs fundamentally from the ground of peoplehood in Israel. He has become the basis of an anti-Judaic gospel.

There is no way to retrace this historical path and assume literally the stance of Jesus as prophetic critic and messianic proclaimer in the Judaism of his day. If the 970 million Christians were suddenly to apply to reenter Judaism, the 14 million surviving Jews would certainly not know what to do with us. Rather we must reconstruct the stance of Jesus in a way appropriate to our own historical condition.

There are two elements needed to correct the anti-Jewish reading of Jesus' criticism of religion. On the one hand, we must recognize that prophetic criticism is always internal criticism, springing from loyalty and commitment to the true foundations of the people whom you criticize. It is fundamentally distorted when it becomes the repudiation of another people who are no longer your own. Therefore, whatever is valid in the denunciation of legalism and hypocrisy in the Gospels must be appropriated by Christians as self-criticism. We must translate "scribes" and "Pharisees" into such words as "clerics" and "theologians." Since most of us who have that opportunity are ourselves clerics and/or theologians, it should be evident that what is being criticized is not Christianity, or even Christian leadership, but certain false ways of setting up leadership that crushes the message of the gospel. We might remember that Jesus himself was called rabbi by his apostles.

This kind of internalization of the gospel critique of religion is already quite common in Christian theology and preaching. Many liberal and liberation theologians, such as Hans Küng or Leonardo Boff, put particular emphasis on this denunciation of false religion precisely for the purpose of criticizing fossilized hierarchical religion within their own communities.

However, this internalization of the gospel criticism will not overcome the anti-Judaic stereotype unless we are willing to concede to the Judaism of Jesus' day the same religious validity that we attribute to our own Christian faith. Surely we expect our own religion, not only to survive, but to be purified through such criticisms. If Hans Küng does not think he becomes anti-Catholic because he denounces hypocritical hierarchicalism in the Roman Catholic Church, then he should not assume that Jesus fundamentally departs from the ground of Torah and Israel when he makes a similar denunciation of false teachers.

This second principle is seldom observed by Christian scholars. Again and again we find theologians, not just conservatives, but theologians on the left, who are happy to use the Gospel denunciations to critique legalistic tendencies in their own community. And yet they continue to write as though these bad traits, which are only distortions of *their* faith, are somehow *generic* to Judaism. Indeed, such anti-Judaism becomes reasserted and defended by liberal and liberation thinkers as though the purging of the shadow side of their own faith still demanded the Jewish scapegoat as its point of reference.

This negative projection of Christian self-criticism onto Judaism cannot be corrected without a positive appreciation of Judaism, of the rabbinic tradition, and of Jesus' place in the Judaism of his time. Christians must discover that leaders of the Pharisaic schools, such as Hillel, were making some of the same interpretations of the Law as did Jesus; i.e., that love of the neighbor is the essence of the Law. Christians must correct the stereotypic use of the word "Pharisee." Only then will Christian exegetes and preachers be prepared to translate the New Testament language into the same kind of nuanced appreciation of Jesus' Judaism that they would expect to convey about their own Christianity; namely, a religion that contains the possibilities both of prophetic vision and of institutional deformation.

The Schism of Particularism and Universalism

Christians have seen their faith as the universal religion, superseding the particularism of Judaism. Paul's "neither Jew nor Greek" is seen as the great breakthrough from tribal religion to the religion of universal humanity. Christianity fulfills the messianic promise of the ingathering of all nations, as opposed to the particular identification of Israel with one people and one land. It is true that particularism, even in the Hebrew scriptures, sometimes becomes ingrown ethnocentricity and animosity to others. But what has been less apparent to Christians is the way universalism can become imperialism toward other peoples. Christianity has seen itself as the *only* valid, redemptive identity. All other religions are spurious, demonic, and lacking true relationship to God. To be saved, all must incorporate themselves into the one true human identity, the Christian faith. Even modern liberal theologians, such as Bultmann or Küng, speak of Christianity as "authentic humanity" without asking whether this means that all other peoples have an inauthentic humanity. The missionary who viewed non-Christians as "devil-worshipers" did not always avoid translating this theological judgment into a racial judgment on the inferior nature of non-Christian peoples. The zeal to conquer and subdue often went hand-in-hand with the command to convert all nations.

Such imperialist universalism fails to be authentically universalist. It actually amounts to absolutizing one particularism. In this respect Christianity can learn something from the very different way in which Judaism has understood universalism. Judaism has seen itself as having a universal mission to enlighten other nations about higher religion, expressed particularly in monotheism and their basic code of ethics; i.e., the Noachic code, as distinct from the Torah. Although Judaism is open to the true proselyte, it has not seen its mission primarily as conversion of others. This is both because Judaism sees its special characteristics as given to a particular people, and also because it believed that the "righteous Gentile" could be saved in his or her own religion. Conversion to Judaism is not necessary for salvation. These views lay the basis for a self-limited particularism that, potentially, recognizes the rights of other peoples to define their own identity and relation to God in terms of their own religious culture.

True universalism must be able to embrace existing human pluralism, rather than try to fit every people into the mold of religion and culture generated from one historical experience. Only God is one and universal. Humanity is finally one because the one God created us all. But the historical mediators of the experience of God remain plural. There is no final perspective on salvation available through the identity of only one people, although each people's revelatory point of reference expresses the universal in different contexts. Just as each human language points more or less adequately to universal truths, and yet is itself the product of very particular peoples and their histories, so religions are equally bearers of universal truth, and yet are particular in form. To impose one religion on everyone flattens and impoverishes the wealth of human interaction with God, much as imposing one language on everyone steals other peoples' culture, and memories. If there is a messianic end-point of history that gathers up all these heritages into one, it can only happen through incorporating them all, not through suppressing them all in favor of the experience of one historical group. In order to be truly catholic, Christians must revise the imperialistic way they have defined their universality.

The Schisms of Law and Grace, Letter and Spirit, Old and New Adam

Classical Christian theology brought together two kinds of dualism, one inherited from apocalyptic Judaism and the other from hellenistic philosophy. The apocalyptic dualism divided the messianic people of the new age from a fallen and apostate history. The Qumran community, for example, saw themselves as the messianic Israel of the age to come, over against the apostate temple and unconverted Jewish nation.

In the hellenistic Jewish philosopher Philo we see an exegesis built on the dualism of letter and spirit, outwardness and inwardness, body and soul. Philo himself did not translate this into a sectarian type of Judaism. Rather he wished to give a sacramental understanding of Jewish laws and rites whereby the outward observances point to higher spiritual and universal truths. He did not negate the laws and rites themselves, but enjoined fellow Jews to observe them with a new understanding.

The apocalyptic dualism of the messianic community against the apostate Israel fostered polemical sectarianism. In the Dead Sea sect only the Qumran covenanters are regarded as the true Israel that will inherit the promises in the age to come. The apostate Israel will be cut off and thrown into the pit of fire. Yet the Qumran sect remained intra-Jewish. It sought to convert fellow Jews into its own community. Christianity originally probably shared this type of Jewish messianic sectarian perspective. But, as it became progressively Gentile and alienated from fellow Jews, it translated this intra-Jewish sectarianism into an anti-Jewish sectarianism. Judaism became the alien religion and nation that has been superseded and negated by God.

The absorption of the Platonic dualism of letter and spirit into the sectarian apocalyptic dualism allowed Christianity to define itself over against the old Law and covenant. The old covenant and Law is seen as only the "fleshly foreshadowing" of a redemptive truth that is now fulfilled on a higher spiritual plane in Christianity. Christianity is seen as superseding Judaism, not only historically, but morally, and even metaphysically. Judaism becomes only letter, fleshliness, and carnality, compared with Christianity as spirit and grace.

The fallacy here lies in confusing the break between two historical peoples with the theological line between history and eschatology. The distinction between ambiguous historical existence and perfected messianic life is imported into history to define the line between two peoples and two historical eras. Israel as the harlot people (which, in the Old Testament, expressed critical historical realism) is used by Christianity to depict the Jews only in negative terms over against the perfectionist version of the church as the messianic bride of Christ. This results in a mystification of Christian reality. Christians project the shadow side of human life on to the Jews as the symbol of the fallen and unfulfilled side of existence. We find here a polarization of a dialectic, which makes sense when applied to one community but creates a completely distorted perspective, both for oneself and for the others, when split into two peoples and two "eras."

Judaism is not only letter, any more than Christianity is only spirit. All religions, indeed all human cultures, are a complex dialectic of letter and spirit, faith and law. Religious renewal always wishes to make the content, the inner experience, predominant. But this never takes place without mediating community structures, patterns of prayer, creed, liturgy, ethics, and community life. Christianity has certainly not been without all these embodiments. Indeed, ironically, its constant search for renewal of the inward experience means that it has proliferated far more "embodiments" of itself than any other historical religion. But it has also mystified the relationship between the spirit and the institutional embodiments, either trying to deny historical embodiments, as in spiritualist, charismatic movements, or else idolizing its historical, institutional form as perfect and divinely given. Christians have yet to develop a realistic account of the relative, yet necessary, relationship between inner content and historical embodiment.

Christian churches have also tended to proliferate supersessionist views of historical relationships. Not only is Christianity seen as superseding Judaism, but each renewed church sees itself as superseding its parent church. The new church is the true church of spirit and faith, replacing the old church of dead letter and rote ritual. This same supersessionist pattern has also been projected into the secular doctrine of progress. Progressive peoples see themselves as superseding and rendering obsolete the unprogressive. We must criticize this supersessionist view of historical relationships.

We can indeed value and affirm those breakthrough experiences of human life that allow new groups to arise and to develop historical identities that are authentic and fulfilling. But this does not mean that the religion or nation from which the group has departed becomes superseded in some absolute way. The former group may be discovering, at that very same time, an equally authentic way of renewing themselves on the basis of their traditional symbols and forms. Thus Christianity, at the very period when it was shaking the dust of Judaism off its sandals, failed to notice that Judaism was undergoing a creative renewal. Indeed it was the Pharisees who refounded Judaism after the demise of the temple and laid the basis for rabbinic Judaism.

Christianity, as much as Judaism, continues to live in a dialectic of fulfillment and unfulfillment. Christianity, in the Resurrection, looks back to a foundational experience that expresses hope and conquest of defeat. Judaism, which did not participate in this particular experience, continues to renew itself out of the experience of the Exodus, which mediates much the same message. For each, the hope mediated by the breakthrough experiences of liberation is the basis for a continued struggle for the final resolution to the riddle of history, which is as much ahead of us Christians as it is ahead of the Jews.

The supersessionary pattern of Christian faith distorts both Jewish and Christian reality. We should think rather of Judaism and Christianity as parallel paths, flowing from common memories in Hebrew scripture, which are then reformulated into separate ways that lead two peoples to formulate the dialectic of past and future through different historical experiences. But the dilemma of foretaste and hope remains the same for both. For both live in the same reality of incompleted human existence itself.

The Key Issue: Christology

The anti-Judaic patterns of Christian theology were, and are still today, tied to a dogma of fulfilled messianism. So it is not possible to rethink these anti-Judaic patterns without questioning their christological basis. Two steps in this critique of Christology are necessary. First, Christians must formulate the faith in Jesus as the Christ in terms that are proleptic and anticipatory rather than final and fulfilled. Jesus should not be said to fulfill all the Jewish hopes for the coming Messiah, which indeed he did not. Rather, he must be seen as one who announced this messianic hope and who gave signs of its presence, but who also died in that hope, crucified on the cross of unredeemed human history.

In his name we continue to proclaim that hope, and also to begin to experience its presence. But, like Jesus, we also do that under the cross of unresolved human contradictions. The final point of reference for the messianic advent still remains in the future. Its unambiguous arrival still eludes us. Here and now we, as much as the Jews, struggle with unresolved history, holding on to the memory of Jesus' resurrection from the grave as the basis for *our* refusal to take evil as the last word and *our* hope that God will win in the end.

This proleptic understanding of Jesus' messianic identity is familiar to Christian exegetes. It has been particularly renewed in liberation theologies. It is the exegesis that best translates the New Testament experience. Jesus' message is falsified when it is translated into a final fulfillment that is spiritualized and institutionally lodged in the past.

Second, we must see Christology, not only as proleptic, but also as paradigmatic. We must accept its relativity to a particular people. This will be a more difficult principle for many Christians to accept, but it is equally inescapable. The Cross and the Resurrection are contextual to a particular historical community. These are breakthrough experiences that found *our* people, that mediate hope in the midst of adversity *for us*. But this does not mean these are the only ways this may happen, or that other people may not continue parallel struggles on different grounds; namely, the Jews, for whom the events of Jesus did not become paradigmatic events, and for whom the Exodus and the Torah serve as the memory and the way.

Some Christians will see such contextualizing of the Christian symbols as totally unacceptable. For them, Jesus as the only name that may be named on earth and in heaven is absolute. I can only say that our two thousand years of human experience do not allow that assertion to be taken literally. He may indeed be the only name *for us*. But other names continued to be named and do not fail to bear fruit. Nor does it seem to me that the power of Jesus' name will become less if we cease to use that name to deny the validity of other peoples' experience of God through other means. Indeed, only when we cease to use Jesus' name to negate other peoples' experiences of the victory of life over death, can the name of Jesus cease to be a name that creates alienation of Jew from Christian, Christian from non-Christian. Then we can begin to find in our differing ways of mediating hope in the midst of defeat new possibilities of human solidarity.

3
The Question of Politics and Religion in America

Political Awakening

I developed a political consciousness relatively late by some standards. During my undergraduate years I barely ever lifted my nose beyond the fifth century. When my college friends were rallying around Adlai Stevenson in 1956, I still did not know whether I was a Democrat or a Republican. I remember discoursing on political options with favorite relatives at the beach in Mexico. They were ardent Goldwater fans and were trying to persuade me to be likewise. But the more they talked, the more I experienced an unspoken inner dissent. My marriage in 1958 to Herman Ruether helped make me more political. At least I now read the morning paper rather than just the classics. While my graduate studies also continued to focus on the world of classical antiquity, my college church life was bringing

me into contact with the issues of peace and racial
justice. Once exposed to these issues, I seemed
instinctively to gravitate to the Left. Or, to put it another
way, once the question of injustice in the structure of
American society was made evident, there was no
option for me except to make some judgments and
commitments.

The Civil Rights Movement

A watershed experience for me certainly took place
in the summer of 1965. A group of students, organized
by the college chaplains at the Claremont colleges,
decided to work for the summer in Mississippi with the
Delta Ministry. Ironically enough, we crossed the
Mississippi border in our beatup cars just in time to hear
of the explosion of the Watts riots back in Los Angeles.
Obviously we did not need to travel half way across the
country to find the problem of racism. Nevertheless,
this period in Mississippi was a momentous learning
experience, despite the naïveté with which we may have
started out. For the first time, I, as a sheltered
middle-class white, experienced America from the
other side. I learned to see my base in the black
community and to look with fear on carloads of whites
or white policemen. I had church doors slammed in my
face, and saw white storekeepers spread out across a
drug store in battle formation because I was with blacks.

One of the major projects that summer was the
Mississippi Child Development Group that was setting
up Head Start programs for preschool children. Head
Start, for them, was not just an end in itself, but also a
means of broad-based community organizing. In order
to receive a Head Start program, the community itself
had to organize to support it. Once organized, a

community might go on to address other needs, such as sanitary facilities. The project hoped to leave as many communities as possible with a continuing infrastructure for self-development rather than just one-shot largesse from the federal government. I joined this project and traveled around Mississippi.

On the day we arrived in Vicksburg the program was giving health examinations to the children from surrounding towns. Small black children who had never been outside their neighborhoods were being bussed in, wide-eyed and sometimes terrified by the clinic and doctors. I helped one team of young Jewish doctors from New York City give shots, and was amused by their valiant efforts to soften their harsh Eastern urban accents into a Southern drawl to reassure the children. A local black teen-ager was instructed by the doctors in some of the simpler techniques and empowered to help. He immediately assumed an air of competence and professionalism as he took up his tasks. One wonders if that chance to play doctor for a day might have led him to seek the drawn-out and expensive education that is necessary in our society for official medical credentials.

In other areas of our travels we encountered more frightening evidence of white hostility. We arrived in Greensboro shortly after the Delta Ministry couple there had narrowly escaped a shotgun attack through their bedroom window. On one occasion we crossed out of our territory to visit Bogalusa, Louisiana, where the Deacons for Defense had been organized to protect the black community from the Ku Klux Klan. For weeks there had been major Klan rallies in the countryside, while the Deacons nightly patrolled the black community against nightriders. I and my companion attended one of the rallies being held in the church to organize the people. As we emerged from the church we saw the building surrounded by white policemen. The Deacons threw a cordon of protection around the two of us and escorted us to a safe area away from the police.

The identification of the police with the whites against the blacks was so evident it did not even need to be discussed. They were, in effect, the soldiers of an occupying army. Back at our headquarters in Beulah, we regularly posted an all-night watch to guard the campus against white nightriders. Indeed, one carload had recently ridden through and sprayed the buildings with gunshot. Our only defense was to ring a bell, if such an event occurred, to warn the workers to take cover under beds and away from open windows.

One of our main projects that summer was organizing blacks to come out and vote for the civil rights bill that would, among other things, protect their voting rights. During that period I decided to travel to the other side of the state to visit aged relatives of my father. I knew they lived in an antebellum plantation that was reputed to be haunted. My father had told us tales as children about the lady in white that trailed her flowing garments across the garden and the man in the tall black hat who appeared and chatted with visitors from time to time. There was also the noise of sewing from what had been the second-story sewing room in Civil War times, and a piano that played at night. This was something not to be missed.

Once we arrived in the neighborhood, we found that local blacks knew the old house well and directed us up a shaded forest road. Suddenly behind us appeared a car with the Stars-and-Bars on the license plate. Inside were two women in their 70s whom I easily recognized as relatives. They looked exactly like my aunts Sophie and Mary, but they were Cousins Cara and Lady Armstrong. Once identified as Robin's daughter, I was quickly accorded full hospitality. After lunch they escorted me around the house, showing its interesting features. The house had been built around 1820 by an ancestor of French Huguenot extraction, who made an effort to reproduce in roughhewn timbers the elegance of a French chateau. Medallion paintings crowned the corners of the ceiling in the rococo style. The portraits of various relatives on the walls were identified. "This is Cousin . . . , he fought with Stonewall at . . . ," and so forth.

I soon discovered a peculiar trait of my cousins' speech. Although the two women had been born at the turn of the century, they consistently spoke as though they were their own ancestors. Pointing to a side exit, Cousin Cara declared, "We had intended to put a porch on this side of the house to match the porch on the other side. We had an architect all lined up, but then the war came, and we never did build that porch." What war? The Civil War! Time had stood still here. The living descendants of the white plantation masters lived on as if frozen in the decade after the Civil War when the soldiers were returning and the slaves had run away. The antebellum South was still normative for their world. Although I did not see any actual ghosts, I discovered something more peculiar . . . living ghosts. At tea Cousin Cara declared that she was quite comfortable with the family ghosts. They were, after all, her own people, and she expected to join them and live on in the house after her death . . .

Sinister shadows filled the room where we sat. We discovered that there were two brothers in the family.

The four members of the household had recently gone to
vote against the civil rights voting acts (the same one we
were organizing to get passed). One brother had been so
distraught at recent civil rights activities that he had had a
heart attack and died at the polls. Another brother,
Cousin Trooper, had taken to the men's quarters and
hadn't appeared downstairs for a week. As we sat
chatting at tea, the brooding presence of the surviving
brother somewhere in the upstairs of the old house
hovered over us. Needless to say, nothing was explicitly
said about just why "Robin's daughter" happened to be in
Mississippi in the summer of 1965. That would have been
ungenteel. But the cousins were not fooled.

At one point, while showing me the rose window at
the curve of the grand staircase, Cousin Lady turned.
Waving a delicate pink hand, she declared, "If any of
those civil rights workers come around here, we are
going to drive them right out of this world . . ." The
steel hand flashed in the velvet glove. In a moment's
insight I pictured this diminutive lady watching a
lynching with approval from afar. It was with relief that
my companion and I emerged from the old house and
the leafy gloom of the country road and returned to the
human world of the Delta Ministry. In our journey back
in time we had glimpsed something of the deeply
buried roots of racial hatred, aggravated by a century of
resentment at an old way of life spurned and shattered.

After leaving Mississippi, I returned to California
and spent some time working in Watts. There one could
recognize the institutionalization of racism in its urban
setting; the systematic lack of decent schools and
community facilities, again white police as a hostile
occupying army, in what might outwardly appear to be
a pleasant neighborhood of one-story bungalows.

In 1966 my husband and I and three children left California for jobs in Washington, D.C. For me it was a homecoming, because I had grown up in the Radford house in Georgetown until I was sixteen. But I returned to a different city—one I had never known as a child and from which I had been carefully sheltered—the world of black Washington, the real silent majority of the nation's capital.

I was lucky enough to find a job teaching theology at the School of Religion of Howard University, where I remained for ten years (until 1976). These were critical years, not only for civil rights, but also for the peace movement. Black theology had begun to develop and was gingerly being adopted, even by some of the traditional educators of the black church. One could also see the generational split created by the new movements of black power that challenged the old strategies of survival and advancement of the Negro middle class. Sometimes one could see the older generation afraid of being outclassed by the new generation. Sometimes one could recognize the older people fighting for solid values, respect for all people regardless of race, good grounding in the three r's over against what they saw as the fast-talking hucksters that got white attention but ultimately would not serve the black community well.

It was a struggle in which I could contribute little, except to be sure that my students knew, not only something of Augustine and Calvin, but also of Cone and Fanon; that they knew that Augustine's suppression of the Donatists had something to do with the suppression of a native African church and with how the Afro-American church had arisen as a rejection of the racism of white Christianity. Helping bring Dr.

Larry Jones to provide new vigorous leadership to the school was perhaps my most important involvement. But, by that time, I also knew that I should move on to another setting, for the issue of sexism along with racism could not be raised by a white woman, but only by a black woman with full faculty credentials. Fortunately after my departure just such a woman was hired.

The Peace Movement and Anti-Imperialism

The decade of my work in Washington also saw the peaking of the peace movement. It would be hard to count how many marches I participated in; how many sing-ins, pray-ins, and die-ins won me brief stays in Washington jails during that period. Always it seemed like some reliable Jewish lawyer was on the spot to bail the Christians out of the clink. Much of this antiwar effort for me went on through church-related groups; St. Stephen's and the Incarnation Episcopal Church, a center for many of the good things going on then; also the Community of Christ, an ecumenical, covenanted community; and the Community for Creative Non-Violence, mostly Catholic radicals. One lived in a constant atmosphere of political awareness that made any other part of the country appear asleep, although today, after Carter and now Reagan, most of that community of activists in the nation's capital has been dis-employed and is dispersed.

For me the most important role of the peace movement was to lift the question of intergroup injustice to a systemic and global level. Martin Luther King had started that toward the end of his life, and had been condemned as diversionary. One began to put together the links in a global system of Western colonialism and imperialism that stretches back four hundred years. The triangle of trade that linked Europe, Africa, and the Americas was one of slave labor and extraction of rich resources under exploitive conditions. The gold extracted from Mexico and Peru traveled in galleons toward Spain, was stolen in fast ships by the British, and ended in banks in London or Amsterdam. On this capital Western industrialization had been financed.

The same pattern of dependency, exploitation of cheap labor, and colonization of resources—metals, oil, fertile land—continues in more masked forms under neocolonialism and hides under what is euphemously called development. The militarization of Western nations, particularly the United States, the policeman of Western neocolonialism, is inextricably linked with the protection of this empire. This is the reality that lies under the myth of anticommunism and the defense of "democracy." The geopolitical tension goes on between East and West; the economic struggle between North and South. When "democratic governments" prove unable to defend Western hegemony over the labor and resources of the Third World, they are readily replaced with fascist military states, armed and trained to suppress their own people. So much for our defense of "democracy." The slogans of liberalism become a facade to justify a very different reality.

This lesson, learned with difficulty in Southeast Asia, also illuminated American policy in Africa and Latin America. The antiwar movement could not end when the last marines took flight from the roof of the American embassy in Saigon. It was now transmuted into a much longer and more difficult struggle of anti-imperialism. This consciousness began to turn me increasingly in the seventies toward Latin America. Here was a culture interwoven with my own family biography. My mother had been born in Monterey, Mexico, and spoke Spanish fluently from childhood. As early explorers in California, the Ords had inter-married with the Mexican governor's family in Santa Barbara. My mother could still recall visiting Aunt Rebecca as a teen-ager and being sternly told to speak no English in her household.

Latin America was not only the prime area of American neocolonialism, it was also the hidden reality of internal colonization within our own borders. The annexation of half of Mexico (a third of the United States) is one of the most unacknowledged crimes in American history. It is being repaid by a constant infiltration from South of the border of a Latino under-class. This under-class has remained largely invisible to white America. How many people, even in Chicago, know that a third of their city is now Latin? Without political representation, often without civil rights, the Latinos form an undercurrent of super-exploited labor, constantly expelled, and yet just as constantly allowed to return to do their needed services, often below minimum wages.

In addition to this pool of menial laborers, there is another Latino presence in America that is smaller and more special, but with an equally important message. This is the exile community who have fled from various repressive regimes in Central and South America, regimes sponsored and armed by U.S. dollars, who come to agitate for their countries' freedom in the very bosom of Babylon. A Chilean, a former labor organizer, now cleans floors in my seminary, teaches seminary students Spanish on the side, and hawks tickets to the

periodic *peñas* organized by the Chilean exile community to support their resistance movement. As I write, it
is the El Salvadoreans that are particularly active,
traveling around to any audience that will hear them
with their film, *Revolution or Death,* trying to show
American audiences the reality of U.S.-sponsored
fascism so carefully concealed in the mass media.

The Question of Socialism

The recognition of structural economic injustic both
within the United States and between this nation and its
dependent allies led me to consider the question of
socialism. As an undergraduate, I had read Marx with
European professors for whom that system of ideas was
a normal part of one's intellectual equipment, so these
ideas were not unknown. But for me, as for most
Americans, a living socialist tradition was something
strange and exotic, associated with "New York Jews"
and the McCarthy witch-hunts of the fifties. It is one of
the misfortunes of American social history that a
mass-based socialist party was destroyed at the end of
the First World War by a combination of government
suppression and Leninist subversion. The resultant
Communist and Trotskyite parties that emerged in the
twenties have remained tiny ideological splinter sects
without roots in the American working class. As a result
we lack a native base for socialist analysis and politics.
This has two effects. It prevents Americans from
recognizing the class structure of our society. Workers
and poor people identify with the ideology of corporate
management and aspire to its goals. Second, Americans
easily cooperate with the suppression of Third-World
liberation struggles in the name of "anticommunism."
The civil rights and anti-imperialist struggles of the

sixties brought a new birth of socialist thought in this
country, including a revival of Christian socialism, but
mainly among intellectuals. This intellectual socialism
remains without a real base among poor and working
people. The racial and feminist issues thus are easily
coopted at a level of middle-class tokenism. Even the
leaders of these movements often fail to recognize the
class nature of their leadership and aspirations. The
integration of talented middle-class blacks and women
into managerial offices becomes the success symbol of
these movements. The fact that these gains fail to affect
the black and brown masses or the vast majority of
working-class women remains unnoticed.

Indeed, the peculiar American form of radicalism
among these movements, black nationalism and countercultural feminism, tend to be hostile to class analysis.
They see this as diluting a race- or sex-based solidarity,
failing to recognize that the reality of class division
makes such solidarity mostly an illusion. The fact that
one of the most disaffected elections in the nation's
history could express itself in a "Reagan landslide"
shows the inability of much of the electorate to
understand their own self-interest and the inability of
the left to communicate an alternative analysis, much
less provide an alternative politics.

My own prescription for a socialism that might have a
chance of making an impact on American life would
include the following: It must be democratic, American,
nonsectarian, and political.

1. *Democratic:* Socialism in this country must clearly
reject the Leninism and Trotskyite dogmatism and
authoriarianism. It must be honest and critical about
the unacceptable character of this brand of communism
in Russia, China, Eastern Europe, and even Cuba,

though it may be sympathetic to some real gains in standard of living for the people in some of these countries. But it must be clear that a dogmatic, authoritarian party that centralizes all power in itself and suppresses real participation or dissent is not an authentic expression of socialism. Socialism must be understood as an extension, not a suppression, of the liberal tradition, an extension from political and cultural into economic democracy. Socialism is not state capitalism, but workers' self-ownership and self-management of the means of production. It means taking back basic control over the economic forces that govern our lives, not surrendering it to a state bureaucracy. Only if socialism is clearly differentiated from this Leninist, state-capitalist tradition, does it have any chance of communicating to the American people as a real response to their needs.

2. *American:* A viable socialism must be American in ideology. It must speak out of the heart of our traditions of democracy, dissent, justice, and community life. It must draw on the liberal, communitarian, and biblical languages that are deep in our soil. It must learn to speak its message in the ordinary folk languages of this country, not with the ideologies drawn from intellectual or "foreign" rhetoric. Although it should be sympathetic to Third-World liberation struggles, it must learn to express this support in a way that does not sound like an attack on most Americans. Rather, it must convincingly isolate the military, corporate, and government leadership responsible for this imperialism from the interests of the masses of the people. It needs to show that the same profit-oriented leadership that exploits Mexican workers also closes plants in Detroit and moves production to areas of nonunionized cheap labor. It

needs to show that this international ruling class does not serve the interests of most Americans much better than it serves the interests of most Latin Americans. In short a new socialism needs to fight a cultural battle in the mainstream of national life to create a new consciousness.

3. *Nonsectarian:* A new American socialism needs to eschew the dogmatism and sectarianism that has marginalized socialist parties into splinter sects since the 1920s. It must be flexible to a number of parallel strategies and broad coalitions. Socialist party-building within the left wing of the Democratic party does not necessarily rule out alternative party-building. There can be two tracks in conversation with each other that might eventually merge. Indeed a mass-based socialist party could probably develop only by simultaneously building a left wing within the Democratic party (the strategy of the Democratic Socialist Organizing Committee, DSOC) and also alternative base organizations that could eventually come together when the Democratic Socialist left wing became large enough to disaffiliate from the limits of its alliance with the present Democratic party.

We must be in conversation with all branches of American socialism. Suspicions between DSOC, Theology in the Americas, and Christians for Socialism that one or the other is "mere" Social Democrat or incipiently Leninist are largely importations from ancient battles foreign to the reality in the past or today. Although dogmatic Leninist modes of organization or ideology cannot be emulated, there can be conversation with many individuals within the ranks of these groups who, so far, have had no place else to go. Most of all, a new socialism must seek alliance with all the existing bases of American radicalism; with neighborhood community organizing; with the environmental movement; with racial minority movements; with the women's movement, especially as that relates to poor and working-class women; to labor unions, especially the new union efforts among disenfranchized workers; with antiwar and anti-imperialist movements. It should develop indigenous leadership to provide alternative strategies when corporations shut down plants and threaten the livelihood of entire towns. It needs a good network among church and synagogue leaders who are often effective links to local communities.

4. *Political:* Finally an indigenous socialism cannot afford to be separatist or utopian. Too much American radicalism spurns "electoral politics" in the manner of "the elect" spurning alliance with Babylon. The results of this were readily seen in the recent election when the political aggressiveness of the New Right easily wiped out liberal senators and representatives. The large numbers of people involved in radical concerns had virtually no political organization to counter this strategy. It is said that the New Right has taken a page from left coalition-building of the sixties. If so, it is time for the left to take a page from the strategy of the right. Single-issue constituencies of the left need to be gathered together in a unified strategy; so, for example, all people concerned with environmental issues would have been alerted to just what a Reagan victory would mean—the likely appointment of a hard-right anti-environmentalist as Secretary of the Interior.

A broad coalition of American radicals needs to be ready to defend the tenure of liberal members of congress on the national and state level, and to begin to elect their own candidates for these offices. But they should not concentrate exclusively on the national level, although this is not to be ignored. They need to translate neighborhood and community organizing into electoral strength for local candidates for city and state office. This has to be the base for the electoral strength of national candidates. The fact that Latinos and blacks are the vast majority of the city of Chicago, and yet are largely without city officials to represent their interests, shows the failure of community organizing to translate itself into effective efforts to take political power. The gerrymandering that prevents minority neighborhoods from being represented as integral communities needs to be challenged on the level of city government. In short, American radicals need to come home to genuine political thinking and acting, if they are not to see their concerns swept away by a new American fascism that marches under the Bible and the flag.

The Biblical Roots of Liberation Theology

The idea that the Bible is a political document or that Jesus had a political message is often disputed, not only by conservative Christians, but also by liberals. The message of salvation is seen as speaking only to individuals on a spiritual and other-worldly plane. The more sophisticated neoorthodox form sees the gospel as confronting "all" political systems and "leveling them" all before the righteousness of God. The gospel is thus seen as having a judgmental message toward political systems, but in a way that does not allow any one to be affirmed as better or "closer" to the Kingdom than another. While this position often claims to recapture the political message of the Bible, it also results in a basically apolitical and status-quo position, since no divine sanction can be given to a preference for different social order from the present one, all social orders being equally sinful.

In reality, theology has never really been apolitical. There has always been either a hidden or overt politics in every theological system. Its message is either one that sanctions the existing system or calls for disaffiliation from it in the name of an alternative reality, either directly or indirectly. There have been Constantinian systems that directly identify an existing political system as the expression of the divine will. There have been other theologies whose spiritualism or transcendentalism acts primarily as a dissuasion to any social or political criticism, and so functions to support the status quo covertly. Other theologies directly judge existing systems as evil or call for a disaffiliation from them in the name of alternative communities of faith. Thus the question is not whether a theology is political or not, but rather what kind of politics it mandates. Only a theology that denounces all forms of impoverishment (including spiritual impoverishment) and calls for a more just and mutual society, as God's mandate for creation, are in line with the normative message of biblical hope.

Today Christian conservativism and fundamentalism have thrown off the mask of apoliticism and are revealing their real political options. These options turn out to be capitalism, war, and fewer civil rights for poor people, women, and minorities. Many liberal church leaders are dismayed by this politicization of fundamentalist religion. They are so accustomed to using religion to support vaguely progressive social agendas which do not fundamentally critique their own social system and, at the same time, neutralizing the Bible as a message with concrete judgments and hope for contemporary society, that they are left without response in the face of militant right-wing use of the Bible.

In appropriating the political dimension of biblical messianic faith, one must steer between several false options. On the one hand, there is simply the appropriation of the message of the Kingdom as fulfilled in one's own political establishment. To dissent from it is to fight against God's established order. Both Stalinists and American triumphalists have versions of this idolatry. On the other hand, those who correctly see the message of the Kingdom as a denunciation of present injustices may fall into a revenge theology that simply projects God's anger against others, and fail to see it as a message which includes themselves. Once in power, they easily become new triumphalists. Yet the effort to avoid these two pitfalls must not lead us into that transcendentalizing or neutralizing theology that fails to direct a genuine message of criticism and hope to the concrete contemporary social and political situation. This cutting edge of the prophetic word operates as a gift of discernment. Hence it cannot be translated into a dogma or fixed formula. The appropriate word has to be rediscovered in new ways in new situations.

I believe that this is exactly the process that we see going on in the biblical prophets and also in Jesus' use of the message of the Kingdom. Jesus' announcement of the Kingdom is not Zealot revenge politics, but neither is it a neutralizing transcendentalism, as so many Christian commentators would have it. It strikes at the heart of the political corruption, but in a way that brings that message home to his own society rather than just projecting it against the enemies of Israel. It is in Latin American liberation theology that I think we are discovering a new starting point for linking biblical messianic hope with the mission of Jesus.

Liberation theology does not start first with a dogma about God's becoming "man," or divine epiphany. Neither does it start from the communal experiences of the resurrected Lord or of worship or of the kerygma of Jesus, as in Bultmannian existentialism, or of the teachings of Jesus, as in liberal moralism. Rather, liberation theology focuses first on the historical Jesus, specifically on his liberating praxis. It is these deeds of Jesus that reveal the meaning of his person and his message.

Fundamental to Jesus' liberating action is his preferential option for the poor. Here liberation theology sees itself directly grounded in the mission of Jesus. The following of Christ must start with this critical option, which is not a matter of charity of the rich for the poor. It is not, after all, the church who "goes unto the poor." Indeed if the ruling classes, and the church, which has been a part of the ruling classes, had opted for the poor, there would be no poor. Their existence reveals the option of the ruling classes against the poor, whom they have chosen to oppress and exploit in order to create a world secure for their own profits and privileges.

It is not we, the privileged (Jews or) Christians, but God who chooses the poor. God, through his prophet Jesus, acts in history by preaching good news to the poor, the liberation of the captives, the setting at liberty of those who are oppressed (Isa. 61:1-2; Luke 4:18). In so doing Jesus also reveals God's critical judgment against the rich and the powerful, the religious and social elites. The liberation of the poor becomes the critical locus of God's action in history. The movements of the poor can be seen as signs of the Kingdom, as the places where God is acting in history. John the Baptist's question about Jesus' messianic identity is answered by pointing to this liberating praxis: "the blind receive their sight, and the lame walk, and lepers are cleansed, and the deaf hear, the dead are raised up, and the poor have the good news preached to them" (Matt. 11:4; Luke 7:22).

Since it is the rich who have deprived the poor of all hope, God opts for the poor in order to right the wrongs of history. The poor and the despised will have a priority in the Kingdom. Having nothing in this world, they will be particularly receptive to the good news, while the rich man will go sadly away. The pious and the educated will take offense at the messianic prophet, for they have been used to gaining status and power over others through their education and religious obser-vances. For this reason it is said that the prostitutes and tax collectors will go into the kingdom of God ahead of the religious elites, the scribes and Pharisees (Matt. 21:31).

This has nothing to do with romanticization of the outcasts, or the assumption that the poor are righteous simply because they are outcasts. The tax collector, Zacchaeus, who was both despised and an exploiter in the imperial system, responded to Jesus by declaring that he would give half his goods to the poor and restore fourfold to those he had defrauded. It is for this response that Jesus declares, "Salvation has come to this house," and "He also is a son of Abraham. For the Son of man comes to seek and save those who are lost" (Luke 19:10). Thus those who are rich, even the exploiters, have hope if they hear the good news as a call to give up their false wealth and join Jesus in solidarity with the poor.

But the respectably privileged refuse to hear this message. This is why it is so hard for them to enter the Kingdom. The message for them is "Those who would be first must become last and servant of all." Jesus exemplifies in his own life what it means to become a servant of all and to give one's life as ransom for many. Basically, following Christ means to follow this way of life in the concrete contexts of the social conflicts of one's time.

Liberation theology restores the kingdom of God to the center of the Christian message. Like Jesus, the message of the church is to announce the Kingdom. Christology and the church must be understood in relation to the Kingdom, which means the overcoming of every evil, the wiping away of every tear. One cannot divorce social and physical evils, such as poverty, nakedness, homelessness, lameness, blindness, and disease, from spiritual evils, as though the social and material level was inferior and unimportant. Jesus manifests his liberating work in the realm of physical afflictions first of all. It is precisely in this physical and social realm that spiritual bondage and liberation of people is being manifested. To see that the world is full of the outcast and afflicted is to see that the world is presently in bondage to the Prince of Darkness. To see these afflictions being overcome is to know that the redeeming finger of God has come upon us. It is in this sense that the Kingdom is already "in our midst." It is not "within us" in the sense of an inward spiritual Kingdom as distinct from an outward and social one (Luke 17:21).

For liberation theology the Kingdom is neither something that evolves from the present social system, nor is it unrelated to real social changes in history. It comes about through liberation, through the freeing of people from bondage to sin and evil, and so is experienced as an in-breaking of grace. It cannot be incarnated completely in any particular social system. It transcends the limits of social systems, even revolutionary ones, and judges their inadequacy, pointing to the further hopes still unrealized. Yet this does not reduce all social systems and situations to the same level. Some situations are "closer" to the Kingdom than others, not in an evolutionary progressive way, but in the sense of signs and mediations of the Kingdom that better disclose what God's intention is for humanity.

In our present world, when we see a society where a few rich families own almost all the land, where they suppress all protest with guns and tanks, where they manipulate religion and education to justify this exploitation, then we are far from the Kingdom. But when we see the vast majority rising up against these evils, overthrowing the police state, beginning to create a new society where the hungry are fed, and the poor are able to participate in the decisions that govern their lives, then the Kingdom has come "close." It is in this sense that liberation theologians would say that some social situations and even some social *systems* are closer to the Kingdom than others. Some situations disclose greater justice and mutuality; some systems allow for greater justice and mutuality.

This does not mean that closeness to the Kingdom is an assured possession of any particular system. A liberating situation can degenerate into an oppressive one. Those who made good changes on behalf of the people can turn their power to gain more and more privileges for themselves, and the last state of that house can become worse than the first. Merely claiming democratic or socialist ideology does not assure that the things claimed will be done, any more than claiming to be Christian means one is a real follower of Christ. Closeness to the Kingdom is a matter of concrete reality, not ideology or institutional privilege. It is a matter of discerning the realities of bondage and the realities of liberation that are actually taking place. This is why those who discern signs of the Kingdom are prophets and not merely sociologists.

Nevertheless it is possible, in the midst of the limits and transitoriness of human existence, to make societies that are more liberating and less oppressive, and hence closer to the Kingdom. To deny this is to deny all efficacy to God in history, to make the world solely the kingdom of Satan. The opposite of God's kingdom is not "man's" kingdom, but Satan's. Both God's kingdom and Satan's kingdom are human realms, societies of this world. The task of the follower of Christ is to move human society a little farther from the power of Satan, the rule of alienation and oppression, and closer to God's kingdom, a society of peace, justice, and mutuality.

By restoring the Kingdom to the center of the gospel, liberation theology also throws into question much of the language of finality that the Christian church has been wont to use about Jesus. We cannot speak of Jesus as having "fulfilled" the hopes of Israel, for these were hopes for the kingdom of God. That has not been established on earth in any final or unambiguous form, either in the time of Jesus or through the progress of the Christian churches or nations. We cannot speak of Jesus as having overcome all evil or having delivered us from all sin, as though this were a final and definitive possession needing only to be appropriated in faith and applied to some inward and invisible reconciliation with God. Such language mystifies history and betrays Jesus again, to the extent that it turns us away from the concrete realities of good and evil in human life and teaches us that we can be saved apart from these realities.

The Kingdom was present in Jesus' time in those concrete signs of liberation, those acts of healing and love that manifested the breaking of Satan's power over human life. But it was also absent in Jesus' time. The elites refused to hear him. His own disciples misunderstood him and sold him out. The Romans crucified him. The powers and principalities showed in Jesus' death that they were still in command. Christian faith, as resurrection faith, arises through a refusal to take these facts of the victory of evil as the last word. In the face of the assassination of prophets, Christian faith reaffirms that life and liberation are possible and God will win in the end. Jesus, the crucified prophet, thus becomes the name in which we continue to reaffirm this faith, his own faith, that the Kingdom is at hand. But we affirm this faith, not simply by verbal affirmations, but by following his liberating praxis and putting ourselves, as much as possible, in the place where he put himself, as ones who are willing to be last and servants of all.

But this means Christians, the church, can become followers of Christ only by knowing that they are, first of all, descendants of the betrayers of Christ. As successors to the apostles, the church descends from those who sold Jesus for thirty pieces of silver and betrayed him three times in the courtyard of the high priest. We are descendants of those who pressed Jesus to seize power, to use miracles to display his authority, and thereby to establish a new realm of domination where we could sit on his left hand and on his right. "Get thee behind me, Satan," Jesus said to Peter, the prince of the apostles, and the prince of the tempters and betrayers. The church continued to betray Christ by using his name to establish a new kingdom of domination, to rear up new classes of princes and priests, and to justify the subjugation of women, slaves, and the poor. The kingdom of Satan is thus doubly entrenched in history since Satan may wear the robes of Vicar of Christ and use the cross of Jesus as his scepter.

Liberation theology becomes possible only through a profound repentance of the church. It is therefore significant that liberation theology arises particularly from the church of Third-World peoples, from the churches that were planted in the lands of black- and brown-skinned peoples by uniting the cross of Christ with the sword of the Conquistadores. It arises from peoples who know what it means to be colonized; colonized religiously, as recipients of an imposed religion from Counter-Reformation Europe used as a tool of pacification of the poor; colonized culturally as people whose language and culture were replaced by those of the conquerors; and colonized politically as peoples whose vast poverty and political subjugation is a tool of an international system of profit.

Yet liberation theology arises in Latin America from people who know that they are heirs of their Spanish fathers and not merely their Indian mothers; from peoples whose Catholic Christianity and European languages are a heritage to be claimed and transformed, not merely repudiated. It was through this colonial culture that they also heard the good news of Jesus and learned to discover the real meaning of his message at long last. Latin American liberation theology arises from a church that is, first of all, a repentant church, a church that knows it came as a part of a system of exploitation and acted for much of its history as a tool of domination.

As Catholic Christians, such liberation theologians as Boff, Sobrino, and Miranda do their thinking in profound recognition of the ambiguity of the church from its beginnings. They cannot skip over any part of this history or claim innocence for it. They have to deal with a church that is closed to repentance because of its claim to an inerrancy endowed by Christ himself. They have to look at the way this church sacralized the power of Rome by merging the kingdom of Caesar with that of Christ. They have to trace through the centuries the way the church has made Christ the apex of a class hierarchy of rich over poor, men over women, masters over slaves, clergy over laity, nobles over serfs, and finally Europeans over Asians, Africans, and Indians. All the evils of the world from which Christ came to liberate us have been taken into the church and sanctioned through the Lordship of Christ. The cross of Christ has even been made the lynching post for Jesus' own people, the Jews.

How then does one discover in this church the gospel as good news to the poor? Because this same church is also the church of Latin America, the church of people who are poor, exploited, and despised, victims of these systems of colonization and dependency. It is by identifying with these people, its own people, the Latin American masses, that the church learns to hear the words of Christ and become a repentant church. This means this church has to speak, not simply of personal sin, but of social sin, of sin as collective and institution-alized violence and greed. Social sin is not just the sum of the sins of individual sinners. It becomes a world that we inherit and that biases our opportunities, either as oppressed people or as privileged people, even before we have been able to make personal choices. This means that even people of good will do evil and profit by evil because of their privileged location in this system. This sense of social sin gives liberation theology a new understanding of the Christian doctrine of inherited sin, not as sin inherited through biology, but through society.

Liberation theology has to criticize many of the emphases in traditional theology, such as individualism, other-worldliness, the divorce of the spiritual from the social, the imaging of God and Christ as white, male, ruling-class persons. These are not merely intellectual errors, but sins of idolatry and blasphemy. Tendencies of classical theology are recognized as ideological, in the Marxist sense of ideas that justify social injustice. The gospel is thereby turned into bad news for the poor. Christ is made the founder of colonizing empires, and the church becomes an accomplice in oppression.

The repentant church is a church that has profoundly evaluated this evil history and knows that it can be rectified, not by words, but only by deeds, by concrete actions putting its own life on the side of the poor, and critiques these oppressing ruling classes. The church that follows Christ must itself exemplify in its own life his preferential option for the poor. It must be prepared to lose its privileged position in society, to become one of the persecuted, the tortured, the murdered. It must be ready to be a martyr church. For to follow Christ's preferential option for the poor in Latin America means to be ready to follow him into the grave.

The sign of the reign of evil in Latin America is not

merely the reign of poverty, but the reign of death; the heaps of slaughtered peasants who are tumbled into a mass grave because they sought to organize a peasant's union; the bodies of tortured student, worker, and peasant organizers found dumped in fields and rivers. The church in Latin America testifies to its determination to be the repentant church, the church of Christ, not merely by following the poor into their poverty, but also into their death. Lay catechists, priests, nuns, even some bishops, join the ranks of the imprisoned, the tortured, the assassinated. It is from this reality that Latin American Christians speak to Christians of the First World, of Europe and the United States, about what it means to hear and preach the good news of God's preferential option for the poor.

This is why Latin American liberation theologians are often impatient with theologians from affluent societies who cavil at their views and accuse them of fomenting class conflict, teaching the identification of the Kingdom with particular social systems or ideologies, or of being too immanentist. Such judgments fundamentally distort the message of liberation theologians. They are not adverse to refining their distinctions. But, for them, theology must be done, can only be done, by the ones who situate themselves in the reality of oppression, and whose theology is reflection of liberating praxis. Others who do not do their theology from this context are suspect. Unable to understand what is being talked about, their theological objections are often screens against real involvement.

Gustavo Gutiérrez constantly reminds Christians of the First World that the subject of liberation theology is not theology, but liberation. Christ calls us to be about the task of liberation, not about the task of theology, unless that becomes a servant of liberation. There is no neutral theology, any more than there is a neutral sociology or psychology. Theology is either on the side of all by being on the side of the poor, or else it is on the side of the oppressors by using theology as a tool of alienation and oppression. This is why theology in Latin America is a serious matter, a life-and-death matter, and not simply an affair of the academy.

For Latin American Christians, it becomes evident that the real denial of God is not atheism, but idolatry. Many who think they deny the existence of God do so because they reject the abuses of religion. The ones who really deny God are those who use God's name to justify evil.

The meaning of the Cross, of redemptive suffering, also appears in a different light for those who suffer and are killed as part of the struggle for justice. Too often Christians have treated the sufferings of Christ as some kind of cosmic legal transaction with God to pay for the sins of humanity, as though anyone's sufferings and death could actually "pay for" others' sins! Christ's cross is used to inculcate a sense of masochistic guilt, unworthiness, and passivity in Christians. To accept and endure evil is regarded as redemptive. Liberation Christians say that God does not desire anyone's sufferings, least of all Jesus', any more than God desires or blesses poverty. Suffering, death, and poverty are evils. God comes not to sanctify, but to deliver us from, these evils. Solidarity with the poor and with those who suffer does not mean justifying these evils, but struggling to overcome them.

As one struggles against evil, one also risks suffering and becomes vulnerable to retaliation and violence by those who are intent on keeping the present system intact. This is not a question of violence or nonviolence on the part of those who struggle. Nonviolent struggle is no protection against unjust violence in a system maintained by unjust violence. But in risking suffering, and even death, on behalf of a new society, we also awaken hope. The poor learn not to be afraid of those in power and begin to take their destiny into their own hands. Even when the prophets are killed, the struggle goes on. Indeed their very death becomes a rallying point for new energy. In their name people now organize themselves to renew the work of liberation. The memory of their lives becomes stronger than the powers of death and gives people hope that the powers of death can be broken. This is the real meaning of redemptive suffering, of Jesus and of Christians—not passive or masochistic self-sacrifice.

The suffering and death of the just also raises the question of theodicy. Why does a just and all-powerful God permit the good to suffer? If God can deliver us from evil, why doesn't "he" do so? Christians begin to rediscover the stark meaning of the cry of Jesus from the cross: "My God, my God, why hast thou forsaken me?" The messianic prophet has given his life as ransom for many, has preached good news to the poor, has healed the afflicted. But the powers and principalities are not changed. They close in on him and string him up on the gallows of their false justice. As his blood is poured out, he scans the sky looking for the hand of God, but the heavens remain closed. God does not reach down to draw his prophet out of many waters and deliver him from his enemies.

Does the Resurrection allow us simply to deny this cry from the cross? Do we say that Jesus did not really intend this as a cry of despair, that all along he knew

God would raise him up on the third day? Too often Christians use the Resurrection as a way of not taking the unresolved evils of history seriously. We forget that the Cross is not initially a symbol of the victory of God, but of victory for the powers and principalities. We transform it into a symbol of the victory of God only if we reject this victory of evil by continuing Jesus' struggle against it. We should not stifle the cry of Jesus by spiritualizing this victory over death, but, instead, let it continue to ring out from the Cross, from all the crosses of unjust suffering throughout history, as a question mark about the nature of present reality.

Who then is really in charge of history: God or Satan? If we say that God is really the author of this unjust history, that God is merely using it to test us, or that God has abdicated for a while only to intervene later, we make a mockery of the death of martyrs. Perhaps this whole concept of God as omnipotent sovereign is thrown into question by the death of Christ, by the martyrdom of the just. Such a God is modeled after the powers of domination. When we model our God after emperors and despots who reduce others to dependency, then we have a problem of theodicy. But the Cross of Jesus reveals a deeper mystery. The God revealed in Jesus has identified with the victims of history and has abandoned the thrones of the mighty. In Jesus' cross, God abandons God's power into the human condition utterly and completely so that we might not abandon each other. God has become a part of the struggle of life against death. This is perhaps why those who struggle for justice do not ask the question of theodicy. They know that the true God does not support the thrones of the mighty, but is one with those who struggle.

While the church which opts for the poor is primarily

a critic of the unjust powers, it must also be a critic of the project of the poor. In Latin America this is not primarily a question of violence versus nonviolence. Latin Americans are bemused by the obsession of First-World Christians with this issue. In Chile, Brazil, El Salvador, and Nicaragua there exists a situation of total violence. So there is no way to protest or strugggle without evoking violence. Violence is already the dominant reality. The Christian should be with those who suffer rather than with those who inflict suffering, even on the oppressors. But in real struggle, there is no way to keep one's hands clean.

Rather, the point of danger comes when victory becomes possible. How can one avoid the temptation to become the avengers? Is it possible to dethrone the mighty and still redeem them as brothers and sisters? How does one really root out a system of oppression and yet still exercise forgiveness and reconciliation toward those who have tortured and murdered the people? Here is where the Christian character of the struggle is really tested. The Christian begins to understand Jesus' own struggle against messianic temptation. Here the church learns to pray with Jesus, "Lead us not into temptation, but deliver us from evil."

There are two temptations to be avoided. One is simply to seize power in a way that absolutizes one's own victory and identifies it with truth against all critics. In this fashion revolutions quickly turn into new oppressions. The other temptation is to fear becoming involved at all, to prefer failure and death rather than risk real efficacy. God does not desire death, but new life and new possibilities for human community. The Christian, when the time comes, must also risk taking power and seek to use it for service rather than domination.

Yet there are perhaps different roles that are appropriate for church officials at this point. Pope John Paul may be right, although for the wrong reasons. As a rule, priests and nuns should not hold political office. There may be occasional exceptions, as in Nicaragua, where this symbol of Christian solidarity with the revolution is an important bulwark against reaction. Even there, it might be best voluntarily to suspend priestly functions while holding government office. This is not a question of the church's being disengaged from politics, for we are never uninvolved. Rather the Christian who holds church office should use that office primarily to stay at the grass roots with the poorest in their day-to-day needs. In this way the church will avoid the temptation to idealize a particular situation, not to deny the possibility of real change, but to encourage it by keeping the revolution honest.

The struggle is always unfinished; there is still more that needs to be done. It is at this point of the unfinished business of good and evil that the church needs to find its primary point of incarnation. It does so, not to reject the revolution, but to keep it in creative and self-critical struggle. The church can do this with credibility only if it puts its own life into the struggle. As the lesson of Cuba has shown, a church which has not participated in the revolution, cannot be the conscience of the revolution.

4
The Question
of Feminism

Becoming a Feminist

It is hard to trace my awakening to feminism in the same way as my political awakening, because it seems to me that I was implicitly always a feminist, if by being a feminist one means a woman who fights for her full realization and accepts no special barriers to her aspirations on the basis of sexual identity. Even as a small child I can remember an instinctive rejection of efforts to define me in traditional female roles. I recall an incident that took place about the age of eight. I had baked a cake and presented it to the family. My older sister remarked somewhat complacently, "You will make some man a good wife someday." I said nothing, but remember experiencing an automatic feeling of anger and betrayal. In naming my accomplishment in terms of my ability to be someone's wife someday, my sister had thoughtlessly tried to deprive me of my own identity and future as a person. I felt an enormous sense of injustice and insult, without being able to name exactly the cause of my annoyance.

The early sources of this proto-feminism in my family life are intriguing to me. I find it interesting that my oldest sister has always been much more independent and chose eventually to remain single. My middle sister (the one with the "cake" remark) appeared very nonconformist as a teen-ager, but married and became much more conventional in her views of women and religion. Only recently has she begun to try to become autonomous, now that her husband has died and her children are grown. A more rebellious and critical attitude toward the dominant ideologies of the society seems much less congenial to her. Placement in the family perhaps has something to do with this, but finally there is an irreducible element of individual freedom and decision.

Both my father's family and my mother's paternal relatives held very traditionalist, not to say chauvinist, notions about women's place and role. But these became largely inoperative for me by the absence of these male relatives during much of my early child-hood. After my father's death when I was twelve, our family became a community of mother and daughters who had to make it together. In 1952 we moved back to my mother's childhood home in California. There, surrounded by her high school girl friends, I had strong role models of independent women of an earlier feminist generation. Thus, my own placement in the family's history tended to maximize the message of female autonomy and worth that was present in the family circle and minimize those messages that would suggest that my cake belonged to some future husband.

Although my mother never directly challenged the dominant concepts of woman's future destiny as wife and mother, she did little to reinforce them either. As a child we used to play a game about "what you are going to do when you grow up." She would mention all kinds of fantastic possibilities, such as "doctor, lawyer, merchant, or chief," but I never remember once her mentioning wife or mother. This means that in some ways she left me fairly unprepared for the realities of this role. But this also meant that, implicitly, she never gave me the idea that this should be my primary identity.

In middle childhood an important influence on my ideas of myself came from my Uncle David. As a creative man, unfulfilled in his job and without children of his own, he lavished his nurturing energies on his three nieces. At his house we learned the traditions of great art and music. He encouraged each of our talents for music, dance, and the arts. For me the history of Western art is inscribed indelibly as an experiential map through the successive rooms of the National Gallery of Art in Washington, which I traversed many times with him. My implicit assumption that I should be something "creative" undoubtedly owes a great deal to his influence. Aside from my uncle, the role models and authority figures that were really operative in my growing up were almost exclusively women.

In my local Catholic school, those in charge from the top administration down to the classroom teacher were female. There were no boys in our classrooms. Priests were rare and distant figures. Even the divine appeared to be immediately represented by a female, Mary. God and Christ were somewhere in the distance, like the priests, but Mary was the one you talked to if you wanted to pray. So, too, the local Carmelite convent where my mother went to daily Mass. Here was a female world of elderly patients and sprightly nuns. As a child I played in the apple trees of their great yard, got fed an occasional ice cream bar from their freezer, and taught some of the nuns to ride a bike. Once they even dressed me up in their habit and took my picture to send to the register of Catholic women's religious orders, because, as they said, they were all old and they wanted to advertise their order with the picture of someone who was young and pretty.

Although I occasionally glimpsed a narrower and more authoritarian side of nuns, most of my memory is of a cozy, female-run world where I felt myself a favored daughter. The recent radicalization of American nuns and their emancipation of their own communities into creative places of social and feminist advancement allows me to continue this positive association in my contemporary life.

In La Jolla, too, I lived in a world where men were distant and unavailable figures. The role models and means of on-going life lay in communities of women, widows and daughters. When men appeared, back from some distant war or conflict, the women grew silent and respectful. A certain homage was paid to these almost godlike creatures. But one managed effectively on a day-to-day basis without them. Although there were undoubtedly a lot of male figures—priests, male relatives, teachers—who could have given me strong messages about my inferiority as a woman, I didn't encounter them until it was far to late for me to change my assumptions. Even the important influence of brothers, or male peers, who often convey to girls the message of their inferior destiny, was largely absent from my growing up.

These experiences contributed to two basic feelings that I sense had shaped my life long before I consciously reflected on it as a feminist. First, that, as a female, the world ought to be a trustworthy extension of a home that would continue to support and encourage my growth; and, second, that the occasional intrusions of male authority which said me nay lacked real credibility. The priest circling the altar in silken vestments and forbidding access to the altar to women; the musta-chioed military relative who showed up filled with glory and stories from distant wars was an object of some awe and curiosity. But, secretly, one suspected that their aura of superiority was fragile facade, a bombast concealing secret impotence. This impotence of male authority was an unspoken secret between women who carried on, in practice, without them. This perception was probably accentuated for me by the extent of my early segregation. But I suspect that it is actually far more widespread than has been admitted. For endless generations women have paid public deference to male authority while, privately, not really believing in it or counting on it.

Consequently, the occasional challenges to my belief in my unlimited horizons, which I encountered while growing up, I could dismiss rather easily. It was only when I married, at the age of twenty, that I experienced the first major and serious assault upon my well-being as a woman in the world. It astonishes me to think of how thoughtlessly I got married at the end of my junior year in college, a thoughtlessness that was part of the culture of the fifties. By the end of college, women were supposed to get married. An unspoken, but clear, message from the whole society told us that if we failed to achieve this goal by the age of twenty-one, we faced an empty and desperate future. In my junior year of college I met Herman Ruether, then a graduate student in political science at the Claremont Graduate School. We discovered a fair amount of compatibility and almost immediately decided to get married. How we were to plan our lives thereafter in terms of finances, children, my continuing work, went practically undiscussed. Topics about practicalities after marriage were somehow unromantic. It is really quite remarkable that we survived as well as we have under those conditions. Certainly neither church, school, nor family had any words of sane or sensible advice on the eve of such a momentous decision.

Before our marriage, as we were walking together one day, something was said about home and family. Nothing had prepared me for any decisions on the subject, but almost instinctively and without premeditation, I blurted out that I had no intention of simply becoming a housewife. I intended to continue in school for my Ph.D. It was clear that Herc (my husband's nickname) was startled. He assumed that women simply quit and became mothers and housewives after marriage. Fortunately he adjusted immediately to this announcement in good grace and has been very supportive of my education and work ever since.

By some purely accidental bit of luck I picked a husband whose parents were working-class immigrants. Economic survival, particularly during the Depression, had dictated a partnership of two work-lives. Herc's father was a housepainter and his mother a nurse. While he was growing up, his mother often worked the night shift and went to bed in the early morning, and his father got the breakfast and sent the children to school. Herc was accustomed to seeing his father with tee shirt and cigar, flipping the morning pancakes or doing the heavy housework. Such a shared role in the house and the work place seemed normal to him. We thus were able to move very naturally into a pattern where both of us worked on our doctorates and later moved into teaching professions, without some of the strains experienced by those socialized in more middle-class male and female roles, who have tried to change those roles later in marriage.

The chief strains for us came in coping with the irrationality of the Catholic Church's position on contraception. It was evident to me from the beginning that I did not agree with the position and intended to practice child-planning. But the message of the church became positively menacing toward a young couple in that period of American Catholicism. From all sides I received messages that my salvation lay in passive acquiescence to God and biological destiny; that any effort to interfere with "nature" was the most heinous crime. Virtually no criticism of this position was culturally available in the world in which I moved at that time.

Shortly after our marriage, Herc and I visited the crusty old Monsignor of his parish church in Cincinnati. Roughly he informed us that if I wasn't pregnant within a year, he would know that we were "living in sin." I was outraged. It was as though the entire society was suddenly bent on destroying the entire identity and future that I had constructed for myself. The entire system of communities around me was engaged in a passive collaboration with this assault on my being.

I was left to work out my own dissent, both what to do and what it signified. This meant that an enormous amount of energy in the first ten years of marriage went into simply defending myself against this assault, trying to juggle children, marriage, housework, teaching, and graduate work. This struggle has, at least, come out of the closet in the 1970s. Young people have some models and some plans about how to manage. In the late fifties and sixties it was a silent conflict, going on in uncounted households, among people who never communicated this struggle with one another or analyzed its causes.

There is no doubt that I survived this challenge. I finished a B.A., an M.A., and a Ph.D. in the same period that three children were born (1958–64). I even embarked on my first book, which was a criticism of the doctrine of the church (*The Church Against Itself,* Herder and Herder, 1967). I learned that to make it in both worlds with reasonable prowess, women had to learn to work with a rapidity and precision far beyond the wildest expectations of their premarried innocence. It exhausts me even now to think of the enormous energy I have had to put out in order to continue to be a creative thinker and writer, and yet maintain the minimum expectations of family life in our society. Although I might feel satisfaction in the *fact* that I have managed to be a winner in this difficult game, actually, I experience the most acute sense of injustice. It is precisely through this killing reality of the "double shift" that women in modern industrial society are defeated. The promises of equality held out by the official liberalism turn out to be a mirage, designed to make women scapegoat themselves for failures, rather than understand the system that is out to defeat them from the beginning.

It is not surprising then that as I began to move from private struggle to public thought as a writer, one of the first areas I chose to write in was sexuality and reproduction. A major effort was needed to break open the closed Catholic culture on birth control. Although I had been working out my private dissent for some years, an incident in the maternity ward where I had given birth to my daughter Mimi in 1963, galvanized my criticism on the subject.

In the next bed there lay a Mexican-American woman named Assumptione. She had just given birth to a ninth child, born with the cord wrapped around its head. The doctor came to her bedside frequently to report the progress of the child, but also tactfully to recommend that she not return home without some adequate means of contraception. Tearfully the woman described the impoverished conditions into which she would take this ninth child to join its eight brothers and sisters. The house was without central heating. She had to turn on the stove to keep the place warm and was always in terror of being asphyxiated by the fumes. There was little food. Her husband beat her. But, when urged to take some measures against a tenth pregnancy, she could only reply that her priest did not allow her. Her husband also was against it. She told me that her umbilical had hurt during the pregnancy, and she was afraid that this caused the child to have the cord around its neck. I realized with horror that this mother of nine children had no clear understanding of her own physiology. She did not even know that her own umbilical was not connected to that of the child.

This incident precipitated my private struggle and dissent onto the public plane. It became evident that the church's position on contraception was a public crime, causing untold misery in millions of lives throughout the world, among people far less able to defend themselves than I. It was necessary to criticize this policy and the entire sexual ethic and viewpoint on women and marriage that it represented, not just for my own sake, but for those millions of Assumptiones weeping in maternity beds around the world.

So my first feminist writings of the midsixties focused on a criticism of the Catholic views of sexuality and reproduction. Only gradually did it become clear that these views themselves were an integral part of a sexist ideology and culture whose purpose was to make women the creatures of biological destiny. This was connected not only with woman's reproductive role, but her work role in the household and in the society.

Religious Sanction of Sexism

In the late sixties I began formal research on attitudes toward women in the Christian tradition. My classical and historical training was indispensable here. Since I already knew the sources and techniques for getting at the material, it was not difficult to document historic views toward women and sexuality. I have sometimes been asked where I found these sources, as though there were something mysterious about the vast panorama of material on sexism being gradually disclosed through feminist scholarship of the last decade. Of course, writings by women themselves or writings expressing alternative views to the dominant tradition have often been dropped out of the official tradition, and their remains have to be dug up through careful detective work. But the dominant male tradition about women is not hidden at all. It lies right on the surface of all the standard texts of Plato, Aristotle,

Augustine, Aquinas, and the like and its message has been absorbed and taken-for-granted over the generations. It takes a new consciousness to go back and isolate this whole body of material as a problem rather than as normative tradition. The consciousness and methodology for criticism has had to be developed by feminist scholars on their own. No professor ever taught me to recognize it as an "issue."

The first stage of research was simply one of documenting the history of views toward women in the dominant tradition and locating it in the context of the intellectual world-view of the authors. But there was a second stage of discovering the socio-economic and legal context of the actual status of women. This was more difficult, and it is by no means complete. Feminists quickly realize that what men have wanted women to be and what women have actually been able to be and do are two different things. Indeed some of the harshest misogyny of the tradition often occurs when women are escaping from the limits of patriarchy. Periods of particularly violent diatribes against women by male cultural leaders are usually an indication that women are attempting to enlarge their sphere of activity and are colliding with male efforts to prevent it, rather than an expression of consensus about women's place. Vehement dicta forbidding women to speak, teach, lead, or learn in public places is hardly necessary unless there is some movement of women to do these things.

This principle forces us to look at church and synagogue traditions in new ways. The rabbinic dicta of early Talmudic tradition, "Cursed be the man who teaches his daughter Torah," or "He who teaches his daughter Torah teaches her corruption," certainly point to the long tradition of excluding women from the religious learning that led to the rabbinate and that was regarded as the crown of Jewish (male) existence. The similar statement in the New Testament, "I permit no woman to teach or to have authority over men; she is to keep silent" (I Tim. 2:12), similarly shows the exclusion of women from the Christian teaching tradition. These statements became the norm for two-thousand-years of tradition that have sought to keep the definition of the public culture, including the definition of women's nature and role, in the hands of males.

The effects of this exclusion of women from participation in theological education is massive. It means that women are eliminated as shapers of public culture, and confined to passive and secondary roles. Their experience is not incorporated into the official culture. Those who do manage to develop as religious thinkers are neglected or have their stories told through male-defined standards. In addition, the public theological culture is defined by men, not only in the absence of, but against, women. Theology not only assumes male standards of normative humanity, but is filled with an ideological bias that defines women as secondary and inferior members of the human species.

Many examples of this overt bias in the theological tradition can be cited. There is Thomas Aquinas' famous definition of women as a "misbegotten male." Aquinas takes his definition from Aristotle's biology, which identifies the male sperm with the genetic form of the embryo. Women are regarded as contributing only the matter, or "blood," that fleshes out the form of the embryo. Hence, the very existence of women must be explained as a biological accident that comes about through a deformation of the male seed by the female matter, producing a defective human, or woman, who is defined as lacking full human standing.

Women are regarded as deficient physically, lacking full moral self-control, and without capacity for rational activity. Because of this defective nature women cannot represent humanity. Only the male can exercise headship or leadership in society. Aquinas also deduces from this that the maleness of Christ is not merely a historical accident, but a necessity. In order to represent humanity Christ must be incarnated into normative humanity, the male. Only the male, in turn, can represent Christ in the priesthood.

This Thomistic view of women is still reflected in Roman Catholic canon law where it is decreed that women are "unfit matter" for ordination. If one were to ordain a woman it, quite literally, would not "take," any more than if one were to ordain a monkey or an ox. Recent Episcopal conservatives who declared that to ordain a woman was like ordaining a donkey are fully within this medieval scholastic tradition. Whether defined as inferior or simply as "different," theological and anthropological justifications of women's exclusion from religious learning and leadership can be found in every period of Jewish and Christian thought. Sometimes this exclusion of women is regarded as a matter of divine law, as in Old Testament legislation. Christian theologians tend to regard it as a reflection of "natural law," or the "order of nature," which, ultimately, is also a reflection of divine intent. In addition, women's exclusion is regarded as an expression of woman's greater proneness to sin or corruption. Thus, as in the teaching of Timothy, women are seen as second in creation but first in sin (I Tim. 2:13-14).

The male bias of Jewish and Christian theology not

only affects the teaching about woman's person, nature, and role, but also generates a symbolic universe based on the patriarchal hierarchy of male over female. The subordination of woman to man is replicated in the symbolic universe in the imagery of divine-human relations. God is imaged as a great patriarch over against the earth or creation, imaged in female terms. Likewise, Christ is related to the church as bridegroom to bride. Divine-human relations in the macrocosm are also reflected in the microcosm of the human being. Mind over body, reason over the passions, are also seen as images of the hierarchy of the masculine over the feminine. Thus everywhere the Christian and Jew are surrounded by religious symbols that ratify male domination and female subordination as the normative way of understanding the world and God. This ratification of male domination runs through every aspect of the tradition, from Old to New Testament, Talmud, church fathers and canon law, Reformation enlightenment and modern theology. It is not a marginal, but an integral, part of what has been received as mainstream, normative traditions.

However, as one digs deeper one discovers that this exclusion of women from leadership and education is not the whole story. There is much ambiguity and plurality in the views toward women and the roles women have actually managed to play at different periods. Evidence is growing that women in first-century Judaism were not uniformly excluded from study. Some synagogues included them, particularly in the hellenistic world. One thinks, for example, of Philo's strange description of the Therapeutae, an idealized account of a contemplative Jewish sect that spent its life in study of Torah. This community consisted of a double monastery of men and women. Philo assumed that the female community spent its life equally in contemplative study of the Scriptures. Where were Philo's precedents for such an assumption? In this light, the rabbinic dicta against women studying Torah, become, not the statement of a consensus, but rather the assertion of one side of an argument against another practice and viewpoint among other Jews.

Similarly the teachings of Timothy about women keeping silence now appear, not as the uniform practice of the New Testament church, but as a reaction against the widespread participation of women in leadership, teaching, and ministry in first generation Christianity. This participation of women in the early church was not an irregular accident, but rather the expression of an alternative world-view. Women were seen equally as the image of God. The equality of women and men at the original creation was understood as restored through Christ. The gifts of the Spirit of the messianic advent were understood (in fulfillment of the prophet Joel) and poured out on the "menservants" and "maidservants" of the Lord alike (Acts 2:17-21). Baptism overcomes the sinful divisions that divide men from women, Jew from Greek, slave from free, and makes us one in Christ (Gal. 3:28). The inclusion of women in early Christianity expressed a theology in direct contradiction to the theology of patriarchal subordination of women. In this way the New Testament must be read, not as a consensus about women's place, but rather as a conflict of understandings of male-female relations in the church.

This alternative theology of equality—of women as equal in the image of God, as restored to equality in Christ and as commissioned to preach and minister by the Spirit—did not just disappear with the reassertion of patriarchal norms in I Timothy; it can be seen surfacing again and again in different periods of Christian history. The strong role played by women in ascetic and monastic life in late antiquity and the early Middle Ages reflects a definite appropriation by women of a theology of equality in Christ that was understood as particularly applicable to the monastic life. Celibacy was seen as abolishing sex-role differences and restoring men and women to their original equivalence in the image of God. When the male church deserted this theology, female monastics continued to cling to it and understood their own vocation out of it. The history of female monasticism in the late Middle Ages and the Counter-Reformation is one of the gradual success of the male church in suppressing this latent feminism of women's communities. Perhaps then it is not accidental that women in renewed female religious orders in Roman Catholicism today have become militant feminists, to the consternation of the male hierarchy.

In left-wing Puritanism of the English Civil War, the latent egalitarianism of Christian theology again surfaces to vindicate women's right to personal inspiration, community power, and public teaching. The reclerica-lization of the Puritan congregation can be seen as a defeat for this renewed feminism of the Reformation. The Quakers were the one Civil War sect that retained the vision of women's equality and carried it down into the beginnings of nineteenth-century feminism.

Finally, the nineteenth century becomes a veritable hotbed of new types of female participation in religion, ranging from the evangelical holiness preacher, Phoebe Palmer, to Mother Ann Lee, understood by her followers as the female messiah. New theologies that attempt to vindicate androgyny in humanity and God express a sense of the inadequacy of the masculine tradition of symbolism.

Feminists engaged in recovering alternative histories for women in religion recognize that they are not just supplementing the present male tradition. They are, implicitly, attempting to construct a new norm for the interpretation of the tradition. The male justification of women's subordination in Scripture and tradition is no longer regarded as normative for the gospel. Rather, it is judged as a failure to apply the gospel norms of equality in creation and redemption authentically. This is judged a failure in much the same way that political corruption of the church, the presecution of Jews, heretics, or witches, and the acceptance of slavery have been so judged. Not that the "bad" history is to be suppressed or forgotten; it would also be an ideological history that tried to "save" the moral and doctrinal reputation of the church by forgetting what we no longer like. We need to remember this history, but as examples of our fallibility, not as norms of truth.

The equality of women, as one of the touchstones for understanding our faithfulness to the vision, is now set forth as one of the norms for criticizing the tradition and discovering its best expressions. This will create a radical reappraisal of Jewish and Christian traditions, since much that has been regarded as marginal, and even heretical, must now be seen as an effort to hold onto an authentic tradition of women's equality. Much of the tradition regarded as mainstream must be seen as deficient in this regard. We underestimate the radical intent of women's studies in religion if we do not recognize that it aims at nothing less than a radical reconstruction of the normative tradition. These considerations lead feminist criticism to two questions.

What is the vision of social reconstruction adequate to the liberation of women? and What is the new theology or world-view that would express liberation from sexism? I would like to treat each of these in turn, although the limits of this format do not allow for more than a cursory treatment.

Social Reconstruction Beyond Patriarchy

Once something of the full story of women's subjugation under patriarchy and its various ideological justifications has been surfaced, women are often outraged, while men often resist the notion that they should feel "guilty" for this history. Two opposite viewpoints tend to emerge among those who desire change. At one extreme is the view that the whole history was an inevitable expression of a certain stage of social evolution, due to the female role in childbearing and the consequent division of labor between the sexes, possibly also because of the lack of medical technology for birth control. But now, in the modern world, the situation of women's marginalization can be overcome. Things can be changed now, but men cannot be held responsible for the past. Obviously males prefer this viewpoint, but so do some women who are afraid of confrontation with the males in their lives.

The opposite view sees the suppression of women as a great historical crime. Men have deliberately and continually conspired to perpetuate this crime and continue to do so. This reflects the socialization of males into roles of dominance, which they identify with the very essence of their masculinity. Debate then opens up as to whether this socialization of males is nature or nurture. However deep this socialization, is it the psychological reflection of patriarchal social structures and could it be changed once this social base is changed? Or is it a reflection of something essential in male nature? Feminists who take the latter view come close to suggesting that males, by nature, are intrinsically oppressive. Even if it is socialization, it is now so deeply structured into male psychology that women who wish to affirm their full personhood should shun bonding with males. Feminist separatism is the logical expression of this viewpoint. Mary Daly has come closest in theological circles to this view of males as demonic by nature.

My own view lies somewhere between these two extremes. First of all, I believe we must take with full seriousness sexism as a massive historical crime against the personhood of women. This crime was neither biologically inevitable nor the expression of unconscious forces. A social division of labor along lines of biological roles in reproduction undoubtedly took place on the tribal level and corresponded to certain necessities of survival. But it varies considerably in different ecologies. Depending on the relationship of hunting to food-gathering, women often have a preponderant role in food production and initiate many of the productive technologies. The translation of these roles into social power also differs.

The social incorporation of biological roles is a cultural artifact, not a necessity of nature. Particularly once social power is freed from direct prowess in hunting and war and becomes incorporated into legal and cultural superstructures, all biological reasons for eliminating women from leadership roles disappear. The fact that patriarchal societies arise that legislate such marginalization of women is the expression of the will-to-power of a male ruling class, not a biological necessity. This marginalization, moreover, is not maintained by mere unconscious forces, but by the constant reiteration of laws and pronouncements from the guardians of the prerogatives of this male ruling class against women who seek to emerge from its limits. This is a culpable history, in the same way as slavery or racism. Even lack of birth control cannot be used as an excuse, because, in fact, most of the basic principles of contraception have been known for thousands of years, but withheld from women by patriarchal law and religion.

However, one must differentiate between individual and corporate responsibility. Our ethical traditions have developed very little reflection to help us analyze the distinction between individual and social sin. (This itself is a reflection of the ideology of the dominant class. The individualization of sin keeps the dominant culture from having to confront its own particular responsibility for evil.) The social incorporation of unjust roles means that these roles, and the ideologies that enforce them, are passed on from generation to generation. Neither men nor women remember having chosen these roles. This is why it is so difficult for the oppressors to feel personal responsibility for such crimes. The burden of justifying these roles is shifted onto the corporate instruments of the culture. Their justification is lodged with nature or God, which serves as ultimate sanction of the culture.

It is almost impossible for an individual alone to dissent from this culture. Alternative cultures and communities must be built up to support the dissenting consciousness. It can be demonstrated that those who began such dissent in the past had the beginnings of such an alternative community and culture. But even then, if the alternative is not stable and authoritative enough, the individual dissenter is likely to become a mentally unhinged crank, rather than a viable role model of mature personhood. All this means that consciousness is more a product of social relations than we like to admit. Individual consciousness is not merely passive; it is critical as well. But it can only leap a little way ahead of the available social options. It has to be fed by some community that responds to it and moves along with it.

The social base for the birth of feminist consciousness in modern society began with industrialization and the dramatic shift of many of the productive roles formerly exercised by women away from the home. This created a class of women who enjoyed some affluence and culture, but in an increasingly narrow sphere of activity. Feminism began as a protest against this effete existence. Its expression was liberal feminism, a wide-ranging effort over the last two hundred years to break down the legal boundaries barring women from professional education and leadership roles.

Many of these civil rights appear to have been won now in Western industrialized societies. Yet the resistance to the Equal Rights Amendment reflects the refusal to ratify this fact systematically in American society. However, simultaneously with industrialization, there appeared an opposite tendency that subjugated women in a new way. The location of productive or salaried labor exclusively in the public sphere meant that women who remained home became increasingly unskilled and economically dependent. Their dependency no longer needs to be ratified by laws excluding them from education and jobs. It now becomes structural to their marginalization from the workplace. Women are forced to choose between family or work. Housework appears as a new category of unpaid labor, outside the sphere of wage labor. Women in the home are structured into a new level of intensive nurturant activity toward men and children, housework and consumer management, that becomes increasingly complex and culturally demanding as the society more and more points to this activity as the compensation for the alienations of the workplace. Women are blamed for all the failures of men and children to make it in the world.

Women who work are tied to a double shift of domestic and wage labor. They are responsible both for the full span of the male work day, and all the activities associated with the female sphere. Since it is virtually impossible to do both equally well, most women are defeated from the start and accept their economic marginalization and dependency (and become committed to defending the ideologies that justify it). The large number of women who must work become structured into a menial level of low-pay and low-security jobs, or irregular and part-time patterns of employment. The few women who aspire to the full professional careers of the male ruling class necessarily remain exceptional tokens, and often sacrifce marriage or children to do so. They are thereby "punished" as unnatural and unfeminine. Thus, the system of patriarchy keeps itself intact despite the appearance of full acceptance of women's cultural equality and legal rights.

With the modern industrial split of home and work, there also appear new cultural and religious ideologies that justify women's "different" nature. Woman's nature becomes correlated with the nurturant and escapist functions of the home, over against the capitalist work-world. Woman is said to be more religious, spiritual, loving, and altruistic. Men are seen as more strongly sexed (a reversal of the medieval Christian view), more rational and aggressive, but less capable of delicate feelings. Men need women to uplift them, but women retain this elevating role only by remaining in strict segregation in the home. To venture outside the home to play public roles is to coarsen and destroy her feminine nature. Obviously femininity, while presumed to be an expression of woman's biological nature, is a socially precarious possession.

The old patriarchal ideology saw woman as defective and inferior. The new bourgeois ideology replaces inferiority with complementarity. Complementarity is often designed to make woman appear not only different from, but even superior to, males. However, this ideology masks the reality of dependency. This whole concept of femininity is, as Engels recognized, a middle-class ideology. It was only applicable to those women whose husbands could afford a "nonworking" wife. Poor and working-class women fell below the ideology of the "lady" and are not accorded its respect or protection.

Today this ideology has been somewhat modified to accommodate the reality of working women in the middle classes, but the same contradictions between the female domestic role and the work-world remain largely unalleviated. Religious authorities are often the most vehement defenders of the ideology of complementarity and are constantly trying to restore it to normative status in new forms. Both the Vatican and Protestant fundamentalists today have assumed an all-out assault on the woman's movement and its efforts to redefine male-female relations, as well as the relations of family and work.

Feminists are divided about what kind of vision best points toward full liberation. Liberal feminists continue to pursue the agendas of equal rights, equal pay, full access to the work-world and to professional status. Countercultural feminists move in the direction of separate community building, often informed by new principles of ecological life-style. Socialist feminists, on the other hand, see the conflict between women and men as embedded in a hierarchical economic system that divides housework from paid labor and structures women as an unpaid and low-paid labor class at the bottom of both of these systems.

Any feminist solution, whether liberal or utopian, will remain token if the total system is not reconstructed. This demands not only the equality of women with men in the work-world, but also overcoming the conflict between woman's domestic and paid labor roles. The temporal and spatial shape of work itself has to be restructured to allow men and women to participate equally in both worlds. Paternity leaves, shorter full-time work shifts, more flexible work hours, child care on the job, decentralized work places more integrated with living communities, are part of what is necessary. Shared home and work roles cannot be carried out simply as a private struggle between men and women. This possibility must be incorporated into the normative ideologies and social systems. As long as the home-work dichotomy burdens primarily women with a double work load, all hopes for full equality between men and women will be an illusion, even under socialism.

Religious Reconstruction Beyond Patriarchy

There are several trends that appear in feminist religion today. These correspond roughly with the liberal reformist, utopian countercultural, and socialist feminist options mentioned above. Liberal and evangelical feminists believe that equality of the sexes is the real meaning of the Scriptures. This can be made evident by better translation and exegesis. Reformers seek greater access for women to education, ordination, and employment in the churches and synagogues. They assume that Judaism and Christianity are reformable in the direction of equality between the sexes.

Liberation feminists would believe that there is a critical and transforming tradition with biblical faith that can be the basis of the liberation of women and men from sexism. But they see this tradition existing in the biblical and theological past in a more conflictual way. Just as society is divided by class, race, and sexual hierarchies, so the church and theology are divided between an ideological use of religion to sanctify these ruling classes and a prophetic tradition that denounces such use of religion. The salvation message of the prophets points toward a new age when these unjust relations are overcome in a new society.

Countercultural feminist spirituality, on the other hand, would reject the idea that there is any critical or messianic tradition in the Bible or church history relevant to women. What liberation feminists would call patriarchal ideology within the biblical tradition, counterculture feminists declare to be the *only* biblical tradition. They take the most reactionary spokesmen for patriarchal religion at their word when they say that God and Christ are males and only males can represent them. They believe that Judaism and Christianity exist for one purpose and one purpose only, to sanctify patriarchy. Consequently any woman who is concerned to find a feminist spirituality must get out of these religious institutions, purge any attachment she may have inherited to their authoritative symbols, and seek an alternative female-centered religion.

Since there are no established female-centered religions around, countercultural feminists have been engaged in trying to rediscover or create them. Following nineteenth-century anthropologists, such as Jakob Backofen, countercultural feminist spirituality accepts the idea that human society was originally matriarchal. The original human religion, during the long millennia of Stone Age culture, was the cult of the mother goddess and her son, the hunter, which reflected matriarchal society. This religion was subdued by the patriarchal nomadic warriors who conquered the Indian subcontinent and the Mediterranean world in the second millennium B.C.. These nomadic warriors replaced the dominant symbol of the mother goddess with that of the sky god, and subsumed the goddess into the cult of Zeus Pater, or Jupiter, as his subordinate wives, mistresses, or daughters. From the eighth century B.C., to the seventh century A.D. the patriarchal reform religions of Judaism, Christianity, and Islam suppressed the goddess altogether and substituted the exclusive reign of the sky father.

However, countercultural feminists believe that the cult of the mother goddess did not die out completely. It survived underground as a persecuted religion, named witchcraft or devil worship by its patriarchal enemies. The writings of Dame Margaret Murray depict medieval witchcraft as the continuation of the cult of the mother goddess and the horned god. Either in exclusively female or in mixed groups, her followers gathered in secret societies called covens, limited to the mystic number of thirteen. Nine million of these women were sacrificed to the fires or persecution (*sic*). Nevertheless, a remnant of the "true believers" survive into the present world. Today this old-time religion of humanity is being revived in the movement known as Wicca (supposedly the Anglo-Saxon word for "witches"). Followers of the Wicca movement identify with the story outlined above as their religious history and believe that the dominant patriarchal history suppresses the truth about these matters.

Feminist Wicca is believed to be a feminist and ecological religion. It operates on the natural rhythms that connect our bodies with the cosmic body around us. It is not without its ethical code, since truly to bring the human community into harmony with nature is not a personal, but a social, discipline. We must not only rectify our personal life-style, but struggle against the polluting systems of corporate capitalism that proliferate warfare and waste. In her book *The Spiral Dance*, Starhawk (Miriam Simos) teaches spells and incantations and describes how to found one's own coven. But she would reject the notion that such spells are manipulative of others or can be used to do harm. Rather she sees them as ways of transforming one's consciousness, purging oneself individually, or in groups, of depression, anger, and hatred, and putting oneself in right relation to the self, others, and the universe.

Starhawk would also reject female-dominant and separatist forms of Wicca. Such tendencies are understandable compensation for millennia of patriarchal repression of women, but she believes they lack the full redemptive vision of the "craft," and could be as wounding to men as patriarchal religion has been to women. Rather her version of Wicca would include males and females as equals. Through relating to the dual symbols of the goddess and the horned god, females and males find the full androgyny of the human potential. Women find the authority and power and men the gifts of poetry and intuition that have been repressed in them. Both men and women are able to integrate the intuitive capacities of the right brain, which has been repressed into unconsciousness by the onesidedly cerebral patriarchal religions.

The mother goddess is fundamentally an immanent deity, the maternal ground of being of the coming-to-be and the passing-away of all things, the womb of creation. In basing ourselves on her, we base ourselves on the true divine foundations of reality that do not force us to deny our bodies and our material existence, as patriarchal transcendence does. Matriarchal religion allows us to accept the naturalness and goodness of things as they are. It teaches us to "go with the flow," rather than exist as the destructive "rogue elephant" of the world; to see not only all human beings, but the animals and plants, stars and rocks, as our sisters and brothers. American Indian religion and other religions of tribal people also preserve much of this immanentist ecological religion of prepatriarchal humanity.

I have a great deal of sympathy with this option for goddess religion, as well as the communitarian and ecological values that are being expressed through it. In many ways it takes me back to my concerns with the relation of pagan and biblical religious world-views with which I dealt as an undergraduate more than twenty years ago. I have been acquainted for many years with the Great Mother of Syria, the many goddesses of the Mediterranean world; Ishtar, Anath, Isis, as well as the Greek poetic rendition of these figures as Athena, Hera, Aphrodite, and Artemis. When I visited Greece in 1978, I made a special pilgrimage to Eleusis to see the spot where Persephone was "raped" into the underworld, and her mother, Demeter, began the sorrowful quest for her return. My classical professors taught me about matriarchal origins and the conflict of maternal chthonic and paternal sky deities long ago. So these themes are not surprising to me.

Moreover, I retain a fondness for the ancient mother. I would even say that for me the model of divine being has for a long time been more that of cosmic "matrix" than transcendent phallic "act." I reject religious exclusivism. So I have no objection to people finding religious nurture through theophanies of the divine outside the biblical or Christian traditions.

However, when such options are translated into a sectarian faith that declares that feminists must reject all biblical traditions, and identify instead with a counter-myth of the goddess, I have some objections. Much of this countermyth of the goddess is drawn from a very simplistic takeover of what is now an outdated anthropology and history of religions originating in the nineteenth century. Many basic assumptions about the goddess, taken for granted in contemporary feminism, are quite dubious. These are not just superficial matters (such as the great exaggeration of the number of witches burned in the Middle Ages, or the description of the victims only as women), but are fundamentals, e.g., Did any such religion of witchcraft as a goddess-and-nature religion actually exist, or, Did the ancient goddesses represent countercultural feminist values, and a woman's religion, mandating leading social roles for women?

In the ancient Babylonian psalms to Ishtar, the devotees who address the goddess are ruling-class, propertied figures who are concerned with the restoration of their economic prowess and victory over enemies in war and politics, exactly as they are in the Old Testament psalms (which were modeled after Near Eastern psalms). While this might refer to an aristocratic woman as well as a man, the concerns are neither feminist, equalitarian, or countercultural.

This concern with historical accuracy is not a matter of academic quibbling, but rather of true self-knowledge. We do not construct our own identities truthfully if we base them on tendentious falsifications of the human past. But, more importantly, the particular scholarship of ancient religion on which feminist spirituality relies reveals all too clearly its own cultural biases. Historically, this scholarship was a product of nineteenth-century romanticism. Its account of paganism over against biblical religion was woven into that same system of complementarity. Not surprisingly, chthonic religion, the religion of nature-and-earth gods and goddesses, is described in terms of a dualism between femininity and masculinity, nature and civilization, the instinctual and the rational, the immanent and the transcendent.

Feminist spirituality seems to me to have bought into this radical version of romantic complementarity in a separatist and utopian form. There is a lack of critical awareness of the origins of these patterns of thought and their inappropriateness to ancient religion. Not only are alternative, perhaps more helpful, elements of the ancient goddess thus missed, but, more importantly, feminist spirituality identifies itself with a doctrine of woman's nature as intrinsically linked to motherhood, earth, and instinct over against civilization and rationality. This is a formula for marginalizing woman in separatist, utopian sects incapable of addressing realistically the dominant world. It also imbues countercultural feminism with a fundamentally wrong anthropology about women, as well as men. Women, like nature, become the unfallen innocents of history, victimized, but naturally good. One has only to withdraw from the evil world and get in tune with one's bodily and cosmic "lunar" rhythms to recapture paradise.

This kind of romanticism is very congenial to Americans, but it must be rigorously criticized. It sets women apart from men, as possessing a different nature, and projects alienation and evil onto males. This not only falsifies the capacity of women themselves for self-alienation and oppression, but it deprives us of an appropriate way for deciphering the reality of human history.

Feminists have tended to reject biblical ideas of sin, the Fall, and inherited evil because these have been used to scapegoat women. However, it seems to me that this biblical religious pattern should be understood in quite a different way. It means that self-alienation and the transformation of the primal relation of men and women into an oppressive dualism is the root sin upon which the crimes of history have been constructed. There is an alternative reality of harmony—with each other, with God, with nature—that lies underneath this history as our true natures. But it cannot be recovered by retreat of women from men or by fleeing from civilization, but rather by historical repentance. We need a realistic recognition of the capacity for evil as a human (not a male) capacity, and the restructuring of society to maximize the incentives for mutuality, rather than oppressiveness. This biblical pattern of thought gives a critical and transforming tool for dealing with the reality of our own ambiguity in a way that is not possible with romantic ideologies of complementarity. This is why I see in biblical religion a key for any genuine theology of liberation, including liberation from sexism.

This does not mean that the values countercultural feminism seeks to affirm do not have to be reclaimed. The understanding of divinity as goddess, as well as god, the reclaiming of the repressed parts of our psyche, new harmony with nature; all this is a part of that "redeemed" existence we should seek. But it needs to be sought through a liberating, rather than a romantic, escapist project, if we are to be truthful about ourselves and effective in the world.

I do not expect the tension between biblical and "pagan" feminists to be overcome very soon. Indeed, it corresponds to a classical tension within Western culture. This is *not* a dualism between biblical religion and ancient paganism (which was not a countercultural, feminist, ecological religion), but a dualism between the dominant and suppressed parts of the Western consciousness, which is mythically translated into a conflict between the biblical and the pagan, the rational and the instinctual, the masculine and the feminine. The problem with countercultural feminism (and the romantic scholarship on which it relies) is that it takes this projection to be an actual historical description and thus casts people into false options between the dominant and the suppressed consciousness. This tension will probably continue between these two expressions of feminism for some time, until some new synthesis appears that can incorporate them both. I would hope only to keep critical and creative lines of communication open in order to allow for an eventual transforming synthesis rather than just a noncommunicating impasse.

This account of some aspects of my personal and religious journey has entailed many negations as well as affirmations. Unless the relationship of the affirmations to the negations is rightly understood, much of what I have said will be misconstrued. Some will say, "Why be a Christian if Christianity has been anti-Semitic, politically oppressive, and sexist?" Or others will say, "You are not a Christian if you criticize these things."

There are two ways to criticize things, an oppositional and a dialectical way. The oppositional way simply sets up an affirmation as a repudiation of its opposite. The good socialist is set up against the bad capitalist; the good feminist against the bad sexist, and so on. This is part of the same kind of oppositional thinking that has gotten Western thought into so much trouble in the relation of Christian to Jew, Christian to pagan, Protestant to Catholic, rationalist to religionist. We do not need to duplicate this pattern of thinking in leftist form.

I would regard my own mode of thinking as dialectical. I see negation, not as an attack on someone else's person or community, but as a self-criticism of the distortions of one's own being and community. Criticism of these distortions opens up the way for a positive reconstruction of the healing and liberating word of the tradition and capacities of human life. This is the healing and liberating word that I have heard emerge from the Christian tradition, once freed of its distorted consciousness. This is the healing and liberating word I would hope to communicate to others. But this healing and hope is available only through the cross of negation. This cross of negation means both theoretical struggle against false ideologies of oppression and practical struggle against its social consequences. Only through this struggle does one hear a healing word and glimpse an alternative future.